Quilt the SEASONS

24 PROJECTS TO BUILD YOUR SKILLS

Barbara K. Baker & Jeri Boe

C&T PUBLISHING

Dedication

To our families who have patiently supported us throughout the years in all our creative endeavors. They are always there with encouraging words and put up with an abundance of take-out dinners. We couldn't have done it without you!

Text and Artwork © 2004 Barbara K. Baker and Jeri Boe
Artwork © 2004 C&T Publishing

Publisher: Amy Marson
Editorial Director: Gailen Runge
Editor: Cyndy Lyle Rymer
Technical Editors: Carolyn Aune, Sharon Page Ritchie
Copyeditor/Proofreader: Eva Simoni Erb, Stacy Chamness
Cover Designer: Christina D. Jarumay
Design Director/Book Designer: Christina D. Jarumay
Illustrator: Mary Ann Tenorio
Production Assistant: Tim Manibusan
Photography: Sharon Risedorph (quilts) and Jeri Boe, unless otherwise noted
Published by C&T Publishing, Inc., P.O. Box 1456, Lafayette, California, 94549

Front cover: Details from *Spring Flowers, Serenity Winter Wonder,* and *Pumpkin Patch*
Back cover: *Northwoods Quilt*

Attention Copy Shops: Please note the following exception—publisher and author give
permission to photocopy pages 34, 35, 41, 46, 47, 53, 54, 61, 66, 74, 78, 79, 92, and 93 for
personal use only.

Attention Teachers: C&T Publishing, Inc. encourages you to use this book as a text for teaching.
Contact us at 800-284-1114 or www.ctpub.com for more information about the C&T Teachers
Program.

We take great care to ensure that the information included in this book is accurate and
presented in good faith, but no warranty is provided nor results guaranteed. Having no control
over the choices of materials or procedures used, neither the author nor C&T Publishing, Inc.
shall have any liability to any person or entity with respect to any loss or damage caused
directly or indirectly by the information contained in this book. For your convenience, we post
an up-to-date listing of corrections on our web page (www.ctpub.com). If a correction is not
already noted, please contact our customer service department at ctinfo@ctpub.com or at P.O.
Box 1456, Lafayette, California, 94549.

Trademarked (™) and Registered Trademark (®) names are used throughout this book. Rather
than use the symbols with every occurrence of a trademark and registered trademark name,
we are using the names only in the editorial fashion and to the benefit of the owner, with no
intention of infringement.

Library of Congress Cataloging-in-Publication Data

Baker, Barbara K. (Barbara Kearney).
  Quilt the seasons : 24 projects to build your skills / Barbara K.
Baker and Jeri Boe.
      p. cm.
Includes index.
  ISBN 1-57120-232-3 (Paper trade)
  1. Patchwork--Patterns. 2. Quilting. 3. Machine appliqué--Patterns.
4. Household linens. I. Boe, Jeri. II. Title.
  TT835.B253 2004
  746.46--dc21

                    2003012972

Printed in China
10 9 8 7 6 5 4 3 2 1

Acknowledgments

While working on this book we received so much support and encouragement. We wish to extend a heartfelt thank you and appreciation to the following people:

To Stephen, who offered unlimited input, advice, encouragement, and love.

To Mike, for allowing me the freedom to create and explore.

To Elizabeth Phinder, who opened the door to a wonderful opportunity in the quilting world.

To Cyndy Rymer, for all of her encouragement, and for believing that we were talented ladies and would be able to juggle family and quilting.

To our Binding Angels: Sally Names, Judy Ballew, Virginia Mohr, and Michelle Boe, who finished all the bindings on a moment's notice; without them we'd still be stitching.

To Virginia Mohr, Pam Nelson, Mary Ann Lisk, and Nelda Linman, a great group of exceptional quilters, who helped to make the quilts.

To Jean Wells and Valori Wells, who encouraged us and offered excellent advice.

To Wendy Hill, for all her sharing and encouragement that helped us start the book process.

To Rasmussen Farms in Hood River, Oregon, for the opportunity to photograph at their beautiful store and orchard.

To Pastures of God Dahlias in Molalla, Oregon, who enthusiastically opened their farm to us. They graciously entertained us for hours as we photographed their gorgeous dahlias.

To the whole team at C&T, who translated our ideas into a beautiful reality, and lovingly supported us through the process.

To all of our quilting friends, who offered advice and support, and who were also our best critics.

A great thank you to the American Professional Quilting Systems for all their help and support with my machine. All the quilts and projects in this book were lovingly quilted on an APQS. Purchasing a longarm quilting machine opened the door to unlimited possibilities and creativity in my quilting career.

Table of of

April

January

May

February

June

March

Contents

July

October

August

November

September

December

Introduction

A love of fabric, color, and design inspired us to write, quilt, and photograph *Quilt the Seasons*. We share a can-do approach to life, and believe anything is possible. There are no mistakes, just creative expressions and new opportunities. This approach takes the fear out of trying something new. It brings a sense of joyful expectation for the next new project.

Our vision for this book was to share some of our ideas and original designs. We love simple, easy techniques, beautiful colors, and different settings. We offer an array of quilts, wallhangings, table runners, pillows, pillowcases, mantle toppers, and door hangers. Each month begins with a small project that teaches a new technique. You can build your skills with the larger quilt project.

Start by skimming the Essential Instructions chapter, which answers basic questions, provides a quick reference, and explores block construction. Finally, basic finishing skills are presented to help you complete your projects.

The techniques explored in the quilt projects are noted at the beginning of each month. If you are a beginning quilter, start with the beautiful *Spring Flowers* in March, for easy piecing and machine appliqué. Give paper piecing a try in April's *Tropical Dream*, and learn how to create a diagonal setting for your blocks. The *Butterfly Garden* May project is a striking quilt that expands your satin stitch appliqué skills and introduces you to machine trapunto. August's *Summer Harvest* explores Seminole piecing and needle-turn appliqué. Beginning to advanced quilters will love September's *Woven Log Quilt*, a foundation-pieced project made with flannels. If you are an intermediate quilter, take a look at February's *Lover's Knot Quilt*, with its quick and easy piecing techniques that create the illusion of interlocking squares. Learn strip piecing and simple templates with July's *Celebration Quilt*. Work on your paper-piecing skills and learn a dimensional leaf technique with October's *Pumpkin Patch Wallhanging*. January's *Winter Wonder* adds to your basic skills, accurate piecing, and piecing with a specialty fabric. December's *Northwoods Quilt* explores the Log Cabin block, evergreen trees, a diamond border, and machine appliqué. Enhance your color skills and paper piecing with June's beautiful *Serenity Quilt*.

Nothing is impossible if you take one step (or stitch) at a time! So roll up your sleeves, gather your fabric, and get ready to have some fun!

Essential Instructions

Here are some useful tips, tools, and techniques for the projects. They are by no means complete, nor do they explain all of the different ways to do things. Try out different methods until you find one that works for you.

Supplies

Batting: We prefer 100% cotton batting; it is also available in cotton/poly and polyester.

Design Wall: Placing your fabric up at eye level allows you to see how the colors and shapes are working together. Tack a piece of quilt batting or flannel to a flat wall or pin it to a curtain to make a quick and easy design wall.

Fusible Adhesive Web: We recommend a paper-backed stitchable web, which is made to be sewn through, and will not gum up the sewing machine.

> **TIP** *Prewashing your fabric will remove any sizing that can prevent a strong bond between the fabric and fusible web.*

> **TIP** *For hard-to-remove paper backing, gently slip a pin or seam ripper between the paper and fabric and lift up to tear off the paper.*

Iron and Ironing Board: An iron that maintains a high heat, and a wide ironing board are good to have; keep them close to your sewing table.

> **TIP** *Use a dry iron for pressing; steam can distort the blocks or make the fabric pucker.*

Needles: For regular sewing and piecing, use a #80/12 Microtex sharp, jeans/denim, or sharp needle. For decorative sewing, use an #80/12 or #90/14 topstitch or an #80/12 or #90/14 Metallica or Metafil needle. For tightly woven fabrics, use a #70/10 needle. For hand sewing and appliqué, use a size 11 or 12 sharp, and for quilting, use a betweens needle.

> **TIP** *Use an inexpensive pincushion to hold needles. Mark segments on the pincushion with the needle size and type. Mark your place with a colored-glass pin to easily identify the needle that is in the sewing machine.*

Pins: Fine silk pins work best for piecing.

Paper-piecing Paper: Use lightweight copy machine paper or paper-piecing paper.

> **TIP** *To make multiple patterns for paper piecing, staple layers of paper together. Stitch through the layers with an unthreaded needle in the machine. The holes will make it easier to remove the paper.*

> **Note:** If you make photocopies for paper piecing, make sure you check the photocopy's accuracy and use one machine for all copies to avoid size differences.

6. Catch 1 or 2 threads on the fold and insert the needle directly down, then up, catching 1 or 2 threads of the background. Continue stitching about $1/8"$ apart. To end, take two small stitches to the back side. Clip threads.

Needle-turn appliqué

Note: Do not turn under the edge and stitch any part of a piece that will be covered by another appliquéd piece. Simply leave the edge raw on that segment of the piece.

Machine Appliqué

This quick appliqué method uses paper-backed fusible web. It stands up well when washed, and is an easy way to add appliqué details to any project. You can choose many decorative stitches to finish the raw edges. We used the satin stitch, the buttonhole stitch, and the straight stitch.

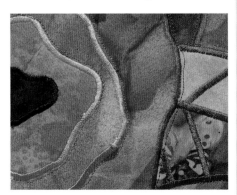

Satin stitch detail on *Butterfly Garden* (page 44)

Buttonhole stitch detail on *Spring Flowers* (page 32)

Note: Before you begin a project, be sure to read the manufacturer's instructions for the brand of fusible web you are using.

1. Look at the pattern, and plan what appliqué piece will go on top and what piece will be tucked underneath another. Try to have the darker fabrics on top of the lighter fabrics to prevent the dark fabric from showing through the light fabric. Add about $1/4"$ to any part of an appliqué piece that will be tucked under another piece.
2. Place the fusible web with the paper side up on top of the appliqué patterns. Trace the lines. Be sure to leave at least $1/4"–1/2"$ between the patterns. Roughly cut out, leaving at least $1/8"$ beyond the traced lines. This ensures that all the edges of the fabric will be fused down.
3. Place the traced fusible web pieces on the wrong side of the fabric and fuse, following the manufacturer's instructions. Cut out the pieces on the traced lines.
4. Peel away the paper backing when ready to fuse. Use a pin to gently lift the paper from the back side.

5. Place the design under an appliqué-pressing sheet, position the individual pieces of each design into place on top of the pressing sheet and fuse together. Allow the design to cool, then peel from the pressing sheet.

6. Position the appliqué pieces on the background fabric and fuse in place.
7. Finish with a decorative stitch around all raw edges.

Decorative Stitching

Before stitching your project, use a sample fabric that has been fused and stabilized to experiment with different stitch widths and densities. Use thread that matches the fabric color, or try black for contrast. Use an open-toe or appliqué foot for a clearer view of the stitching area.
1. Pin stabilizer, or press the shiny side of freezer paper, to the wrong side of the fabric.
2. Fill the bobbin with a lightweight bobbin thread. Loosen the top tension, or use the lightweight tension setting for the satin or other decorative stitches.
3. Draw the threads to the right side of the fabric; secure them with a couple of stitches. Sew the tails into the sewing line. The decorative stitching should cover all raw edges.

4. Pivoting is essential to a beautiful decorative stitch. If your machine has a needle-down position, use it while pivoting, stopping, and starting your stitches. For the inside corners, stitch just past the corner and stop. Leave the needle down in the background fabric. Raise the presser foot, pivot the piece, as shown, and lower the presser foot. Begin stitching the next side.

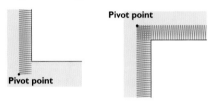

Inside corner satin stitch

5. For the outside corners, stitch just to the corner and stop. Leave the needle down in the appliqué fabric. Raise the presser foot, and pivot the piece, as shown. Lower the presser foot and begin stitching the next side.

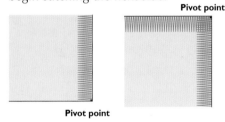

Outside corner satin stitch

6. When stitching outside curves, stop with the needle down in the background fabric, raise the presser foot, and pivot the piece. Lower the presser foot and begin stitching. Pivot as often as necessary to make a smooth curve.

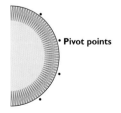

Satin stitch on outside curve

7. When stitching inside curves, stop with the needle down in the appliqué fabric. Raise the presser foot, and pivot the piece. Lower the presser foot and begin stitching. Pivot as often as necessary to make a smooth curve.

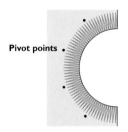

Satin stitch on inside curve

8. Carefully remove the stabilizer.

Borders

Two types of borders are used: a narrow inner border about 1" to 1$\frac{1}{2}$" wide, and a wide outer border, usually 5" to 6$\frac{1}{2}$".

The borders are pieced from strips cut the width of the fabric.

For example, cutting instructions for the narrow inner border may require that you cut 5 strips 1$\frac{1}{2}$" wide. Sew the strips together into one continuous length. Cut the continuous length into 4 strips: 2 for the sides, and 2 for the top and bottom borders.

Note: The border measurements are listed for each project, but measure your quilt top first before cutting these strips! If your quilt top measurements are a little different, you will be able to cut the border strips the correct size for your quilt.

1. Measure the length of the quilt top through the center, and cut 2 strips that length for the side borders. Find the center of the border strip, and pin the center of the strip to the center of the quilt. Pin the ends of the border strip to the quilt top corners. Continue pinning the border to the top. Sew, then press seams toward the border strip.

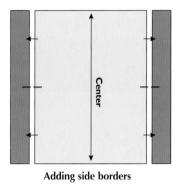

Adding side borders

2. Repeat for the top and bottom borders.

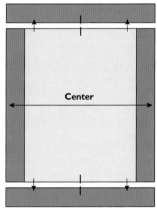

Adding top and bottom borders

Layering the Quilt

You need to layer the quilt top, batting, and backing, then baste them together. Make the backing and batting 4" larger than the quilt top.

1. Place the backing right side down on a flat surface. Secure it with masking tape or clamps. Place the batting on top of the backing. Gently smooth out any puckers. Lay the quilt top over the batting, centering the quilt top on the backing. Spread the quilt out, making sure the quilt edges are parallel to the backing edges.

2. Baste all three layers together. In preparation for hand quilting, baste with white thread. Use a long darning needle, and baste horizontal and vertical lines every 6" to 8". Start in the center and work out to the edges. Baste around the outer edges of the quilt. For machine quilting, use basting spray or safety pins to baste. If you use basting spray, be sure to spray the wrong side of the backing and top fabrics, not the batting. When pinning, start in the center and work out to the edges, placing pins every 3" to 4".

Quilting

Use your favorite quilting method, hand or machine, and choose a quilting design that will add to the texture of your quilt. Look for quilt design books and patterns at your local quilt store; coloring books are also helpful. All the quilts in this book were machine quilted.

Hanging Sleeve

We make our sleeves out of the same fabric as the backing, and baste the sleeve onto the quilt sandwich before adding the binding, so the sleeve is sewn into the binding. The binding is folded from the front of the quilt to the back, and whipstitched to the quilt back.

1. Cut a strip of fabric 8$\frac{1}{2}$" wide x the width of the quilt top measurement minus 2".

2. Turn under $\frac{1}{2}$" on each of the short sides. Press. Turn under another $\frac{1}{2}$". Press, then stitch along the folded edge.

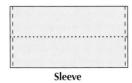

Sleeve

3. Fold the sleeve in half lengthwise, wrong sides together, and press. Baste along the top edge of the quilt, then hand stitch the bottom edge of the sleeve to the quilt back.

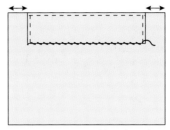

**Baste top edge and hand stitch
bottom edge to quilt back.**

4. Sew the binding to the quilt top.

DOUBLE-FOLD BINDING

We prefer the extra layer of fabric a double-fold binding offers. We also like our bindings to be full of batting. When we trim a quilt after quilting, we leave an extra $\frac{1}{8}$" of batting beyond the edge of the quilt top.

1. Measure the perimeter of the quilt top. The length of the binding strip needs to be the length of the perimeter plus 10" for seams and mitered corners.

2. Cut binding strips 2$\frac{1}{4}$" to 2$\frac{1}{2}$" wide by the length needed. Sew the strips together diagonally. Trim the excess fabric and press seams open.

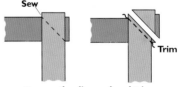

Sew on the diagonal and trim.

3. Fold the binding strip in half lengthwise, wrong sides together, and press. Unfold the beginning edge. Cut a 45° angle and press the edge under $\frac{1}{4}$". Refold the binding.

4. Use a walking foot to sew the binding, starting at the lower left. Begin stitching about 2" from the beginning edge using a $\frac{1}{4}$" seam allowance.

5. Stop stitching $\frac{1}{4}$" from the corner and backstitch.

6. Fold the binding up and away from the quilt, forming a 45° angle. Refold the binding down, aligning the raw edges with the quilt top. Pin. Begin sewing at the edge and continue to the next corner. Repeat for all four corners.

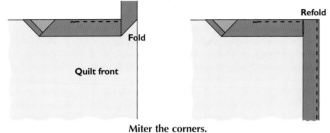

Miter the corners.

7. As you approach the starting point, trim the end of the binding, making sure there is a 1" overlap to tuck into the fold. Stitch the remaining binding to the quilt.

8. Fold the binding over the quilt edge to the back. Hand stitch in place; be sure the binding covers the machine stitching. Miter the corners as shown.

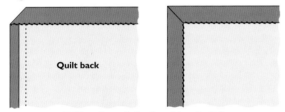

Fold to the quilt back and hand stitch.

Labels

Label your quilts for posterity and to prevent theft! We often use leftover blocks or flowers. List the name, the date, the people who worked on the quilt, an address and phone number, and any other personal information.

Pillow Back Instructions

Knife-edge pillows with an overlapping closure are very easy to make. Be sure to match directional prints before cutting the fabric.

1. Measure the top of the pillow. Cut one piece of fabric $1/2$" larger than the width of the pillow, and $1/2$ the finished length of the pillow + $1 1/2$". Cut another piece of fabric $1/2$" larger than the width of the pillow, and $1/2$ of the finished length of the pillow + $4 1/2$".

2. To form a narrow hem on one edge of each pillow back, press under $1/4$" along the width edge. Then press under an additional $1/4$" and topstitch.

3. Overlap the two backing sections so the top piece overlaps the bottom piece 2"–3", to create a square the same size as the front of the pillow. Pin the sections together.

Overlap pillow backs.

4. Place the pillow top on the back, right sides together, centering it over the overlapped pieces. Trim edges even. Sew around the edge of the pillow, and trim the corners. Turn the pillow right side out, press, and stuff with a pillow form.

An assortment of quilt labels

January

WINTER WONDER TABLE RUNNER

FINISHED PROJECT SIZE: 68" x 17"

FINISHED BLOCK SIZE: 6" x 6"

BLOCKS NEEDED: 4 Nine-Patch, 4 Ohio Star, and 6 Pinwheel Variation Blocks

The sparkle of stars on long winter nights or the beauty of a gentle snowfall reminds us of the wonders of the season. This easy-to-make table runner will add a bit of sparkle to the room. The stars and pinwheels were made using cotton lamé, but could also be made using 100% cotton fabrics. Learn how to quickly and easily strip piece, and make stars and Pinwheel blocks with this project.

Nine-Patch Block   **Pinwheel Variation Block**   **Ohio Star Block**

MATERIALS

Dark blue print: $1\frac{1}{4}$ yards for the background

Light blue print: $\frac{1}{4}$ yard for the Nine-Patch blocks

Yellow cotton lamé: $\frac{1}{4}$ yard or 1 fat quarter for the Ohio Star and Pinwheel blocks

Gold cotton lamé: $\frac{1}{4}$ yard or 1 fat quarter for the Ohio Star and Pinwheel blocks

Pink cotton lamé: $\frac{1}{4}$ yard or 1 fat quarter for the Ohio Star and Pinwheel blocks

Light blue cotton lamé: $\frac{1}{4}$ yard or 1 fat quarter for the Ohio Star and Pinwheel blocks

Binding: $\frac{1}{2}$ yard

Backing: $1\frac{1}{8}$ yards

Batting: 72" x 21"

CUTTING

Prepare the fabric according to the Essential Instructions on page 11.

Dark blue print: Cut 1 strip $2\frac{7}{8}$" wide, then cut into 12 squares $2\frac{7}{8}$" x $2\frac{7}{8}$" for the Pinwheel blocks.

Cut 4 squares $3\frac{1}{4}$" x $3\frac{1}{4}$" for the Ohio Star block triangle units.

Cut 2 strips 6½" wide, then cut into 8 squares 6½" x 6½" for the plain blocks.

Cut 3 squares 9¾" x 9¾". Cut these squares twice diagonally to make 12 triangles for the sides.

Cut 4 strips 2½" wide. From these strips cut 1 strip 2½" x 20" and 2 strips 2½" x 10" for the Nine-Patch blocks; cut 6 strips 2½" x 6½" and 6 strips 2½" x 4½" for the Pinwheels; and cut 16 squares 2½" x 2½" for the Ohio Star blocks.

Light blue print: Cut 2 strips 2½" wide. From these strips, cut 2 strips 2½" x 20" and 1 strip 2½" x 10" for the Nine-Patch blocks.

Yellow cotton lamé: Cut 3 squares 2⅞" x 2⅞" for the Pinwheel blocks.

Cut 4 squares 2½" x 2½" for the Ohio Star blocks.

Gold cotton lamé: Cut 3 squares 2⅞" x 2⅞" for the Pinwheel blocks.

Cut 4 squares 3¼" x 3¼" for the Ohio Star block triangle units.

Pink cotton lamé: Cut 3 squares 2⅞" x 2⅞" for the Pinwheel blocks.

Cut 4 squares 3¼" x 3¼" for the Ohio Star block triangle units.

Light blue cotton lamé: Cut 3 squares 2⅞" x 2⅞" for the Pinwheel blocks.

Cut 4 squares 3¼" x 3¼" for the Ohio Star block triangle units.

Binding: Cut 5 strips 2½" wide.

BLOCK ASSEMBLY

Refer to the Essential Instructions on page 12.

1. Make the 4 Nine-Patch blocks. Sew a 2½" x 10" dark blue strip onto each side of the 2½" x 10" light blue strip. Sew a light blue 2½" x 20" strip onto each side of the 2½" x 20" dark blue strip. Press.

2. Cut the 10" strip set into 4 units 2½" wide. Cut the 20" strip set into 8 units 2½" wide.

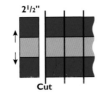
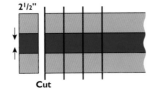

3. Arrange and sew these units as shown in the Nine-Patch Block Assembly Diagram, nesting the seams and pinning. Press.

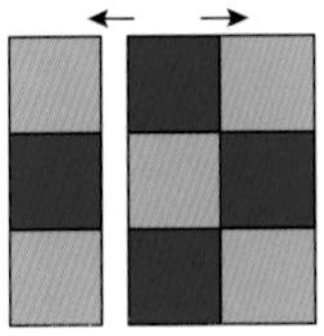

Nine-Patch Block Assembly Diagram

> ◼ **TIP** *If you are using cotton lamé, to avoid melting turn down the temperature of the iron, and do not use steam. Test the temperature of the iron on a scrap piece of fabric before pressing the project.*

4. Make 6 Pinwheel Variation blocks. Use the Quick Piecing Method (page 12) to make 6 half-square triangle units with the yellow cotton lamé and dark blue 2⅞" x 2⅞" squares. Repeat for the gold, pink, and light blue cotton lamé. Make a total of 24 half-square triangle units. Sew the half-square triangle units together into pinwheels. Press.

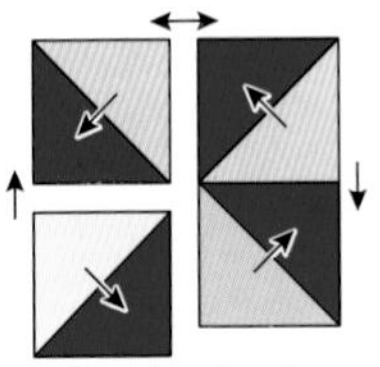

Pinwheel unit

5. Sew a dark blue 2½" x 4½" strip to the side of the pinwheel unit. Press. Sew a dark blue 2½" x 6½" strip to the bottom of the pinwheel unit. Press.

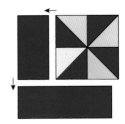

Pinwheel Variation Block Assembly Diagram

6. Make 4 Ohio Star Variation blocks. Use the Quick Piecing Method (page 12) to make 8 light blue cotton lamé and dark blue half-square triangle units using the 3¼" x 3¼" squares. Cut each of the units in half diagonally to make 16 triangle units. Follow the same procedure using the pink and gold lamés to create another 16 triangle units.

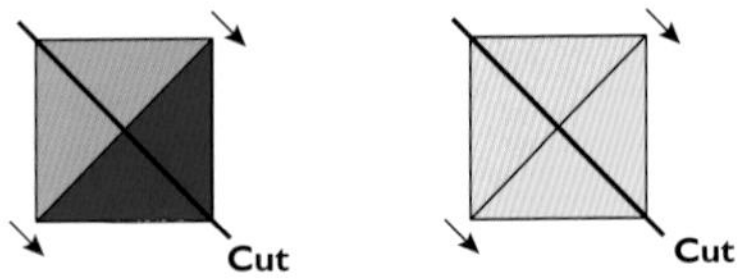

Cut   Cut

7. Sew the triangle units together to make 2½" x 2½" quarter-square triangle units. Press.

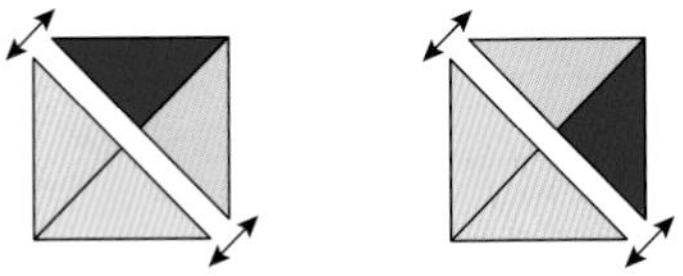

Quarter-square triangle unit

8. Sew the 2 Ohio Star blocks and 2 alternate Ohio Star blocks as shown below. Press.

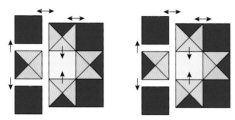

Ohio Star Variation Block Assembly Diagrams

TABLE RUNNER ASSEMBLY

1. Lay out the table runner as shown in the Table Runner Assembly Diagram. Sew the units into rows. Press.

2. Sew the rows together, pinning and matching seams. Press.

FINISHING

Refer to the Essential Instructions on page 17 for general finishing instructions.

1. Layer the backing, batting, and top; baste.

2. Quilt as desired.

3. Bind or finish as desired.

4. Attach a label.

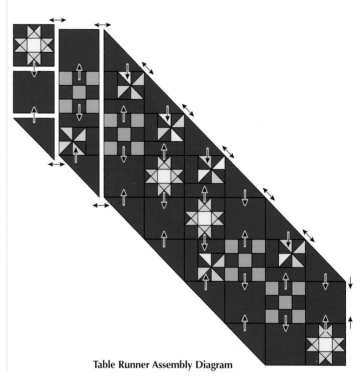

Table Runner Assembly Diagram

WINTER WONDER QUILT

FINISHED QUILT SIZE: 62" x 74"

FINISHED BLOCK SIZE: 6" x 6"

BLOCKS NEEDED: 16 Nine-Patch, 15 Pinwheel Variation, and 22 Ohio Star blocks

This quilt is fun to make any time of the year. It uses 3 simple blocks, and easy piecing techniques. The chosen colors and their placement give this quilt its wonderful look.

FABRIC SELECTION TIPS

The two dark blue background prints should be close in value to add interest to the quilt. The light blue background print should be a noticeably lighter version of the same color. Tone-on-tones will work well for this quilt. Choose cotton lamé fabrics in solid yellow, gold, blue, and pink pastels. Mixing these up is fun and gives the quilt an added sparkle. If the quilt is going to be laundered frequently, substitute 100% cotton fabric for the cotton lamé. It will withstand heavy use better than the cotton lamé.

MATERIALS

Dark blue focus print: 3 yards for the blocks and outer border

Dark blue accent print: 1 yard for the background

Light blue print: $1^{1}/_4$ yards for the background, Nine-Patch blocks, and inner border

Yellow cotton lamé: $^{3}/_8$ yard for the Pinwheel and Ohio Star blocks

Gold cotton lamé: $^{3}/_8$ yard for the Pinwheel and Ohio Star blocks

Pink cotton lamé: $^{3}/_8$ yard for the Pinwheel and Ohio Star blocks

Light blue cotton lamé: $^{3}/_8$ yard for the Pinwheel and Ohio Star blocks

Binding: $^{3}/_4$ yard

Backing: $3^{3}/_4$ yards

Batting: 66" x 78"

CUTTING

Prepare the fabric according to the Essential Instructions on page 11.

Dark blue focus print: Cut 5 strips $6^{1}/_2$" wide, then cut into 25 squares $6^{1}/_2$" x $6^{1}/_2$" for the plain blocks.

Cut 5 strips $2^{1}/_2$" wide for the Nine-Patch blocks.

Cut 7 strips $2^{1}/_2$" wide, then cut into 3 strips $2^{1}/_2$" x $6^{1}/_2$", 3 strips $2^{1}/_2$" x $4^{1}/_2$" for the Pinwheel blocks, and 88 squares $2^{1}/_2$" x $2^{1}/_2$" for the Ohio Star blocks.

Cut 3 strips $2^{7}/_8$" wide, then cut into 30 squares $2^{7}/_8$" x $2^{7}/_8$" for the Pinwheel block half-square triangle units.

Cut 2 strips $3^{1}/_4$" wide, then cut into 22 squares $3^{1}/_4$" x $3^{1}/_4$" for the Ohio Star block triangle units.

Outer border: Cut 7 strips $3^{1}/_2$" wide. Sew into one long strip, then cut into 2 strips $3^{1}/_2$" x $62^{1}/_2$" and 2 strips $3^{1}/_2$" x $68^{1}/_2$".

Dark blue accent print: Cut 4 strips $6^{1}/_{2}$" wide and then cut into 19 squares $6^{1}/_{2}$" x $6^{1}/_{2}$" for the plain blocks.

Light blue print: Cut 2 squares $6^{1}/_{2}$" x $6^{1}/_{2}$" for the plain blocks.

Cut 4 strips $2^{1}/_{2}$" wide for the Nine-Patch blocks.

Cut 4 strips $2^{1}/_{2}$" wide, then cut into 11 strips $2^{1}/_{2}$" x $6^{1}/_{2}$" and 11 strips $2^{1}/_{2}$" x $4^{1}/_{2}$" for the Pinwheel blocks.

Inner border: Cut 7 strips $1^{1}/_{2}$" wide. Sew into one long strip, then cut into 2 strips $1^{1}/_{2}$" x $56^{1}/_{2}$" and 2 strips $1^{1}/_{2}$" x $66^{1}/_{2}$".

Yellow cotton lamé: Cut 6 squares $2^{7}/_{8}$" x $2^{7}/_{8}$" for the Pinwheel block half-square triangle units.

Cut 2 strips $2^{1}/_{2}$" wide, then cut into 22 squares $2^{1}/_{2}$" x $2^{1}/_{2}$" for the Ohio Star blocks.

Gold cotton lamé: Cut 6 squares $2^{7}/_{8}$" x $2^{7}/_{8}$" for the Pinwheel block half-square triangle units.

Cut 2 strips $3^{1}/_{4}$" wide, then cut into 22 squares $3^{1}/_{4}$" x $3^{1}/_{4}$" for the Ohio Star block triangle units.

Pink cotton lamé: Cut 8 squares $2^{7}/_{8}$" x $2^{7}/_{8}$" for the Pinwheel block half-square triangle units.

Cut 2 strips $3^{1}/_{4}$" wide, then cut into 22 squares $3^{1}/_{4}$" x $3^{1}/_{4}$" for the Ohio Star block triangle units.

Light blue cotton lamé: Cut 10 squares $2^{7}/_{8}$" x $2^{7}/_{8}$" for the Pinwheel block half-square triangle units.

Cut 2 strips $3^{1}/_{4}$" wide, then cut into 22 squares $3^{1}/_{4}$" x $3^{1}/_{4}$" for the Ohio Star block triangle units.

Dark blue accent print: Cut 4 strips $6^{1}/_{2}$" wide, then cut into 19 squares $6^{1}/_{2}$" x $6^{1}/_{2}$" for the plain blocks.

Binding: Cut 8 strips $2^{1}/_{2}$" wide.

BLOCK ASSEMBLY

Refer to the Essential Instructions on page 12.

1. Make 16 Nine-Patch blocks following the diagram below. Refer to the assembly method described on page 20. Note that you will need to use full-width strips for your strip sets. Make 2 Dark/Light/Dark strip sets and 1 Light/Dark/Light strip set.

Nine-Patch Block Assembly Diagram

2. Make 15 Pinwheel blocks. Refer to the assembly method described on page 20. Note that the colors in the Pinwheel blocks vary somewhat. This gives the quilt added interest and visual motion. Sew a dark blue $2^{1}/_{2}$" x $4^{1}/_{2}$" strip to one side of 4 blocks, and a $2^{1}/_{2}$" x $6^{1}/_{2}$" strip to an adjacent side of these blocks. Sew a light blue $2^{1}/_{2}$" x $4^{1}/_{2}$" strip to one side of 11 blocks, and a $2^{1}/_{2}$" x $6^{1}/_{2}$" strip to an adjacent side of these blocks.

3. Make 22 Ohio Star blocks. Refer to the assembly method described on page 20.

QUILT ASSEMBLY

1. Lay out all blocks as shown in the Quilt Assembly Diagram.

2. Sew the blocks together in rows. Press.

3. Sew the rows together. Press seams open.

BORDERS

Refer to the Essential Instructions on page 16.

1. Add the light blue side inner borders, then the top and bottom borders. Press.

2. Add the dark blue side outer borders, then the top and bottom borders. Press.

FINISHING

Refer to the Essential Instructions on pages 17.

1. Layer the backing, batting, and quilt top; baste.

2. Quilt as desired.

3. Attach a hanging sleeve, if the quilt is going to be hung.

4. Bind or finish as desired.

5. Attach a label.

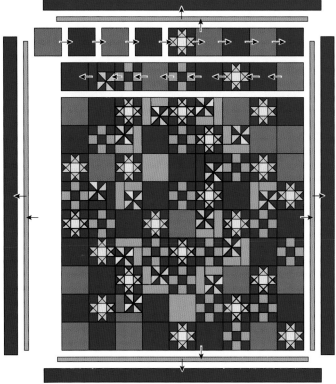

Quilt Assembly Diagram

February

Technique: Strip Piecing and Needle-turn Applique

LOVER'S KNOT WALLHANGING

FINISHED PROJECT SIZE: 37" x 37"

FINISHED BLOCK SIZE: Block A: 9" x 9"; Block B: 4" x 9"

BLOCKS NEEDED: 4 each of Blocks A and B

Lover's Knot is a traditional block with a twist. Combining five colors in the block allows the light colors to recede and the darks to come forward. Careful fabric selection will turn this quilt into a show stopper. This beginner-intermediate quilt uses easy strip piecing, which makes the intricate design very easy to piece.

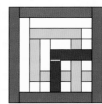

Block A

Connecting Block B

MATERIALS

White: $7/8$ yard for the blocks and Border 2

Pink: $2/3$ yard for the blocks and Border 1

Purple: $1/3$ yard for the blocks, Border 4, and appliqué

Red: $1/3$ yard for the blocks

Green: $7/8$ yard for Borders 3 and 5, and appliqué

Binding: $3/8$ yard

Backing: $1 1/4$ yards

Batting: 41" x 41"

Other materials: Freezer paper, purple and green thread for appliqué

CUTTING

Prepare the fabric according to the Essential Instructions on page 11.

White:

Border 2: Cut 4 strips 1^1/$_2$" wide, then cut into 2 strips 1^1/$_2$" x 24^1/$_2$" and 2 strips 1^1/$_2$" x 26^1/$_2$".

Cut 6 strips 1^1/$_2$" wide, then cut 4 of the strips in half to create 8 half strips 1^1/$_2$" wide for the A and B blocks.

Cut 1 strip 2^1/$_2$" wide, then cut in half to create 2 half strips, 2^1/$_2$" wide for the A blocks.

Cut 1 strip 3^1/$_2$" wide, then cut in half to create 2 half strips, 3^1/$_2$" wide for the A blocks.

Cut 1 strip 4^1/$_2$" wide, then cut into 5 squares 4^1/$_2$" x 4^1/$_2$" for the B blocks and center square.

Pink:

Border 1: Cut 4 strips 1^1/$_2$" wide, then cut into 2 strips 1^1/$_2$" x 22^1/$_2$" and 2 strips 1^1/$_2$" x 24^1/$_2$".

Cut 3 strips 1^1/$_2$" wide, then cut 2 of the strips in half to create 4 half strips 1^1/$_2$" wide for the A and B blocks.

Cut 1 strip 4^1/$_2$" wide, then cut in half to create 2 half strips 4^1/$_2$" wide for the A blocks.

Cut 1 strip 5^1/$_2$" wide, then cut in half to create 2 half strips 5^1/$_2$" wide for the A blocks.

Purple:

Border 4: Cut 4 strips 1" wide; then cut into 2 strips 1" x 28^1/$_2$" and 2 strips 1" x 29^1/$_2$".

Cut 2 strips 1^1/$_2$" wide; from 1 strip cut 1 square 1^1/$_2$" x 1^1/$_2$" for the appliqué. Set aside the rest of the strip for the A and B blocks. Cut the other strip in half to create 2 half strips, 1^1/$_2$" wide for the B blocks.

Red: Cut 4 strips 1^1/$_2$" wide for the A and B blocks.

Green:

Border 3: Cut 4 strips 1^1/$_2$" wide, then cut into 2 strips 1^1/$_2$" x 26^1/$_2$" and 2 strips 1^1/$_2$" x 28^1/$_2$".

Cut 1 square 2^1/$_2$" x 2^1/$_2$" and 4 squares 2" x 2" for the appliqué.

Border 5: Cut 4 strips 4^1/$_2$", then cut into 2 strips 4^1/$_2$" x 29^1/$_2$" and 2 strips 4^1/$_2$" x 37^1/$_2$".

Binding: Cut 4 strips 2^1/$_2$" wide.

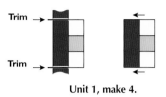

TIP *A reminder: Check your strips every 3 to 4 cuts to make sure the fabric is square. If your strips are not straight, refold the fabric, square the edge again, and resume cutting.*

BLOCK ASSEMBLY

Refer to the Essential Instructions on page 12.

Block A

1. Sew 1 pink half strip 1^1/$_2$" wide between 2 white half strips 1^1/$_2$" wide to make Strip Set 1. Press. Cut this strip set into 8 segments 1^1/$_2$" wide.

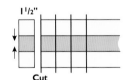

Strip Set 1, cut 8 segments.

2. Sew a purple strip 1^1/$_2$" wide to a segment of Strip Set 1. Press. Trim the purple strip to the same length as the Strip Set 1 segment. Make 4.

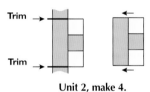

Unit 1, make 4.

3. Sew a pink strip 1^1/$_2$" wide to a segment of Strip Set 1. Press. Trim the pink strip the same length as the Strip Set 1 segment. Make 4.

Unit 2, make 4.

4. Sew a Unit 1 to a Unit 2, making the Center Unit. Press. Make 4.

Center Unit, make 4.

5. Sew 1 purple strip 1^1/$_2$" wide to the Center Unit. Trim purple strip the same length as the Center Unit. Press. Make 4.

Add purple strip. Make 4.

6. Sew a pink half strip 1½" wide between a white half strip 1½" wide and a white half strip 2½" wide to make Strip Set 2. Press. Cut this strip set into 4 segments 1½" wide. Set aside.

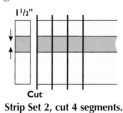

Strip Set 2, cut 4 segments.

7. Sew a pink half strip 1½" wide between a white half strip 1½" wide and a white half strip 3½" wide to make Strip Set 3. Press. Cut this strip set into 4 segments 1½" wide.

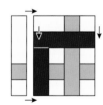

Strip Set 3, cut 4 segments.

8. Sew a segment from Strip Set 2 to the Center Unit and press. Then sew a Strip Set 3 segment to the Center Unit. Press. Make 4. Set aside.

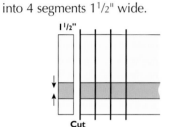

Sew segments to Center Unit. Make 4.

9. Sew 1 white half strip 1½" wide to 1 pink half strip 4½" wide to make Strip Set 4. Press. Cut this strip set into 4 segments 1½" wide. Set aside.

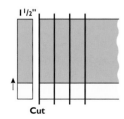

Strip Set 4, cut 4 segments.

10. Sew 1 white half strip 1½" wide to 1 pink half strip 5½" wide to make Strip Set 5. Press. Cut this strip set into 4 segments 1½" wide.

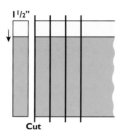

Strip Set 5, cut 4 segments.

11. Sew a 1½"-wide segment from Strip Set 4 and one from Strip Set 5 to the Center Unit. Press. Make 4.

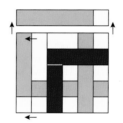

Sew to Center Unit. Make 4

12. Sew 1 white strip 1½" wide to the Center Unit. Press. Trim the strip to the same length as the Center Unit. Add another white strip 1½" wide to the Center Unit. Press and trim.

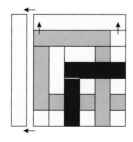

Sew to Center Unit. Make 4.

13. Sew 2 red strips 1½" wide to the Center Unit. Press and trim to the same length as the Center Unit. Sew 2 red strips 1½" wide to the Center Unit. Press and trim to complete Block A. Make 4. Set aside.

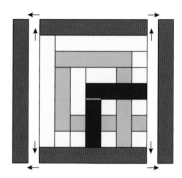

Sew to Center Unit. Make 4.

Block B

Refer to the Essential Instructions on page 12.

1. To make Strip Set 6, sew together 1½"-wide half strips of each of the following colors: red, pink, purple, and 2 white strips in the order shown. Press. Cut this strip set into 4 segments 4½" wide.

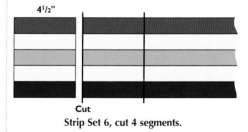

Strip Set 6, cut 4 segments.

2. Sew 1 white 4½" square to 1 segment 4½" wide from Strip Set 6. Press. Make 4. Set aside.

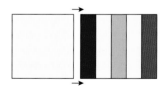

Sew connecting blocks. Make 4.

WALLHANGING ASSEMBLY

1. Lay out the blocks and the white center square as shown in the Wallhanging Assembly Diagram. Pay close attention to the block placement to ensure that the colors will interlock.
2. Sew the blocks in each row together. Press.
3. Sew the rows together. Press.

BORDERS

Refer to the Essential Instructions on pages 16.
1. Add the pink Border 1 side borders, then the top and bottom borders. Press.
2. Add Borders 2, 3, 4, and 5 in the same manner.

APPLIQUÉ

The appliqué shapes are sewn onto the quilt top using the needle-turn method. Refer to the Essential Instructions on pages 14.
1. Position the 4 green 2" x 2" squares on the quilt top as shown in the Wallhanging Assembly Diagram. Pin in place. Appliqué to the quilt top.
2. Position the green $2^1/2$" x $2^1/2$" square on the white center square. Pin in place. Appliqué to the quilt top.
3. Center the purple $1^1/2$" x $1^1/2$" square on top of the green center square. Pin in place. Appliqué to the quilt top.

FINISHING

Refer to the Essential Instructions on pages 17.
1. Layer the backing, batting, and quilt top; baste.
2. Quilt as desired.
3. Attach a hanging sleeve if desired.
4. Bind or finish as desired.
5. Attach a label.

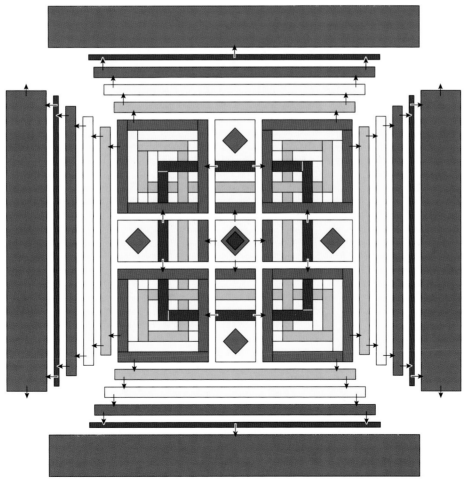

Wallhanging Assembly Diagram

LOVER'S KNOT QUILT

Pieced by Mary Ann Lisk

FINISHED PROJECT SIZE: 64" x 64"

FINISHED BLOCK SIZE: Block A: 9" x 9", Block B: 4" x 9"

BLOCKS NEEDED: 16 each of Block A and Block B

Lover's Knot is so appropriate for February when we celebrate Valentine's Day. Interlocking blocks and beautiful shades of pink, red, and purple set this quilt off. We suggest making this quilt as a special gift for your sweetheart to celebrate special moments.

FABRIC SELECTION TIPS

The fabrics are clear and vibrant in this quilt. There are five basic colors: white, pink, purple, red, and green. The white and red are solids. The pink, purple, and green are blender fabrics, which means they have more than one color in them. The blenders help the color flow from one fabric to another.

MATERIALS

White: $1^5/8$ yards for the blocks and Border 2

Pink: 1 yard for the blocks and Border 1

Purple: $2/3$ yard for the blocks, Border 4, and appliqué

Red: $7/8$ yard for the blocks

Green: $1^1/2$ yards for Border 3, Border 5, and appliqué

Binding: $5/8$ yard

Backing: 4 yards

Batting: 68" x 68"

Other materials: Freezer paper, purple and green threads for appliqué

CUTTING

Prepare the fabric according to the Essential Instructions on page 11.

White:

Border 2: Cut 5 strips $1^1/2$" wide. Sew into one long strip, then cut into 2 strips $1^1/2$" x $46^1/2$" and 2 strips $1^1/2$" x $48^1/2$".

Cut 18 strips $1^1/2$" wide for the A and B blocks.

Cut 1 strip $2^1/2$" wide for the A blocks.

Cut 1 strip $3^1/2$" wide for the A blocks.

Cut 3 strips $4^1/2$" wide, then cut into 20 squares $4^1/2$" x $4^1/2$" for the B blocks and center squares.

Pink:

Border 1: Cut 5 strips $1^1/2$" wide. Sew into one long strip, then cut into 2 strips $1^1/2$" x $44^1/2$" and 2 strips $1^1/2$" x $46^1/2$".

Cut 8 strips $1^1/2$" wide for the A and B blocks.

Cut 1 strip $4^1/2$" wide for the A blocks.

Cut 1 strip $5^1/2$" wide for the A blocks.

Purple:

Border 4: Cut 6 strips $1^1/2$" wide. Sew into one long strip, then cut into 2 strips $1^1/2$" x $50^1/2$" and 2 strips $1^1/2$" x $52^1/2$".

Cut 6 strips $1^1/2$" wide for the A and B blocks.

Cut 4 squares $1^1/2$" x $1^1/2$" for the appliqué.

Red: Cut 17 strips $1^1/2$" wide for the A and B blocks.

Green:

Border 3: Cut 5 strips $1^1/2$" wide. Sew into one long strip, then cut into 2 strips $1^1/2$" x $48^1/2$" and 2 strips $1^1/2$" x $50^1/2$".

Cut 4 squares $2^1/2$" x $2^1/2$" for the appliqué.

Border 5: Cut 6 strips $6^1/2$" wide. Sew into one long strip, then cut into 2 strips $6^1/2$" x $52^1/2$" and 2 strips $6^1/2$" x $64^1/2$".

Binding: Cut 7 strips $2^1/2$" wide.

BLOCK ASSEMBLY

Refer to the Essential Instructions on page 12.

1. Make 16 Block A's. Refer to the assembly method on page 25, using full strips instead of half strips.

2. Make 16 Block B's. Refer to the assembly method on page 26.

QUILT ASSEMBLY

1. Lay out the blocks and the white center squares as shown in the Quilt Assembly Diagram. Pay close attention to the block placement to ensure that the colors will interlock.

2. Sew the blocks in each row together. Press.

3. Sew the rows together. Press.

BORDERS

Refer to the Essential Instructions on page 16.

1. Add the Border 1 side borders, then the Border 1 top and bottom borders. Press.

2. Add Borders 2, 3, 4, and 5 in the same manner.

APPLIQUÉ

The appliqué shapes are sewn onto the quilt top using the needle-turn method. Refer to the Essential Instructions on page 15.

1. Position the 4 green $2^1/2$" x $2^1/2$" squares on the quilt top as shown in the Quilt Assembly Diagram. Pin in place. Appliqué to the quilt top.

2. Center the 4 purple $1^1/2$" x $1^1/2$" squares on top of the green squares. Pin in place. Appliqué to the quilt top.

FINISHING

Refer to the Essential Instructions on page 17.

1. Layer the backing, batting, and quilt top; baste.

2. Quilt as desired.

3. Attach a hanging sleeve, if desired.

4. Bind or finish as desired.

5. Attach a label.

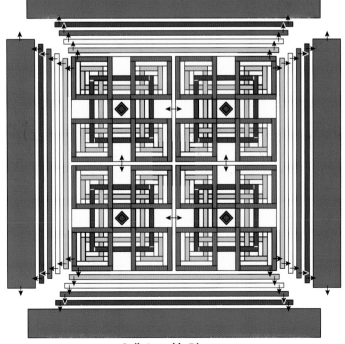

Quilt Assembly Diagram

March

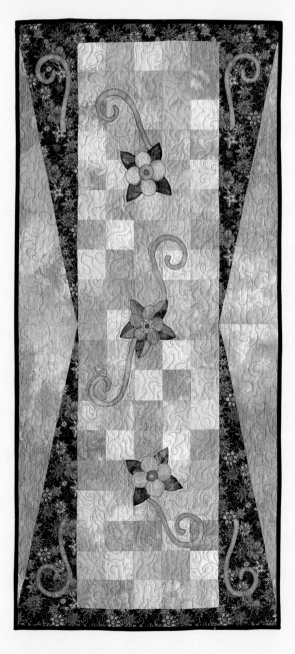

SPRING FLOWERS TABLE RUNNER

FINISHED PROJECT SIZE: 27" x 61"

This table topper will bring the bright cheerful colors of spring into your home. A simple pieced background sets the stage for a bouquet of appliquéd flowers. This is a great quilt for a beginning or intermediate quilter. Buttonhole appliqué makes this a quick and easy project.

MATERIALS

Light green: $2/3$ yard for the background, leaves, and tails

Yellow: $3/8$ yard for the background

Light orange: $3/8$ yard for the background

Pink: $3/8$ yard for the background

Dark orange: $3/4$ yard for the side border, tails, and background

Floral print: $3/4$ yard for the border

Appliqué fabrics: Fat quarters or scraps of the following colors: orange, pink, yellow, magenta, light green, and dark green

Binding: $1/2$ yard

Backing: $1^3/4$ yards

Batting: 31" x 65"

Paper-backed fusible web: $1^1/4$ yards (12" wide)

Other materials: Appliqué pressing sheet, water-soluble stabilizer, and black or decorative thread for the buttonhole stitch

CUTTING

Prepare the fabric according to the Essential Instructions on page 11.

Light green: Cut 4 strips $3^{1}/2$" wide, then cut into 35 squares $3^{1}/2$" x $3^{1}/2$" for the background.

Yellow: Cut 2 strips $3^{1}/2$" wide, then cut into 20 squares $3^{1}/2$" x $3^{1}/2$" for the background.

Light orange: Cut 2 strips $3^{1}/2$" wide, then cut into 12 squares $3^{1}/2$" x $3^{1}/2$" for the background.

Pink: Cut 2 strips $3^{1}/2$" wide, then cut into 19 squares $3^{1}/2$" x $3^{1}/2$" for the background.

Dark orange: Cut 2 strips $6^{3}/4$" wide, then cut into 2 rectangles $6^{3}/4$" x $29^{3}/4$", which will be cut later into the side border triangles.

Cut 1 strip $3^{1}/2$" wide, then cut into 9 squares $3^{1}/2$" x $3^{1}/2$" for the background.

Floral print: Cut 2 strips $6^{3}/4$" wide, then cut into 2 rectangles $6^{3}/4$" x $29^{3}/4$", which will be cut later into the side border triangles.

Cut 2 strips $2^{1}/2$" wide x $27^{1}/2$" for the top and bottom borders.

Binding: Cut 5 strips $2^{1}/2$" wide.

TABLE RUNNER ASSEMBLY

1. Lay out the background squares as shown in the Table Runner Assembly Diagram.

2. Sew the squares in each row together. Press the seams of each row in alternating directions.

3. Sew the rows together. Press.

4. Place wrong sides of the $6^{3}/4$" x $29^{3}/4$" orange rectangles together and cut diagonally to make 4 triangles for the pieced side borders. Repeat using the floral print rectangles.

Note that the wrong sides of the fabric must be together when cutting so the triangles will be mirror images of each other.

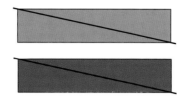

Cut 4 triangles each.

5. Refer to the Essential Instructions on page 13 to sew the side border triangles together. Press. Make 2 L triangle units and 2 R triangle units.

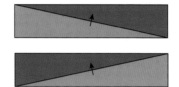

Side border triangle units, make 2 each.

6. Sew 1 L triangle unit and 1 R triangle unit together. Press. Make 2 side borders.

7. Add a side border to each side of the table runner. Press.

8. Add the $2^{1}/2$" border strip to the top and bottom of the table runner. Press.

APPLIQUÉ

Refer to the Essential Instructions on page 15.

1. Enlarge the patterns on pages 34–35 for 1 Flower A, 2 Flowers B, and 4 Tails A and 4 Tails A reversed. Trace the enlarged patterns onto the paper side of the paper-backed fusible web. Cut the required number of shapes from each of the fabrics. Refer to the photo for flower design and placement.

2. Assemble the appliqué shapes for each flower on an appliqué pressing

sheet, and fuse together. Referring to the photo for flower and tail placement, position the shapes on the table runner and fuse in place.

3. Pin water-soluble stabilizer to the wrong side of the table runner. Machine buttonhole stitch around all the shapes using black or decorative thread.

4. Remove the stabilizer by immersing the table runner in water. Press to dry.

FINISHING

Refer to the Essential Instructions on page 17.

1. Layer the backing, batting, and quilt top; baste.

2. Quilt as desired.

3. Attach a hanging sleeve, if desired.

4. Bind or finish as desired.

5. Attach a label.

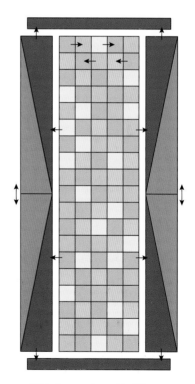

Table Runner Assembly Diagram

FABRIC SELECTION TIPS

Picking a beautiful border print makes your fabric selection easy. Choose a print that offers a broad range of spring colors. Select hand-dyed or solid fabrics for the flowers, leaves, tails, and background. You can fussy cut each appliqué piece from a fabric with multiple colors, to add variety to the flowers, leaves, and background. Be sure to keep the background fabric lighter than the appliqué pieces. The buttonhole stitch in black or matching colors completes the quilt top.

MATERIALS

Light green: $5/8$ yard for the background and tails

Yellow: $3/8$ yard for the background

Light orange: $3/8$ yard for the background

Pink: $3/8$ yard for the background

Dark green: $1/2$ yard for leaves and Road to Oklahoma blocks

Dark orange: $7/8$ yard for the border, tails, and Road to Oklahoma blocks

Floral print: $3/4$ yard for the border and Road to Oklahoma blocks

Appliqué fabrics: Fat quarters or scraps of the following colors: orange, pink, yellow, magenta, and light green

Binding: $1/2$ yard

Backing: $1 3/4$ yards

Batting: 43" x 52"

Paper-backed fusible web: 4 yards (12" wide)

Other materials: Appliqué pressing sheet, water-soluble stabilizer, and black or decorative thread for the buttonhole stitch

Spring Flowers Quilt

FINISHED QUILT SIZE: 39" x 48"

FINISHED BLOCK SIZE: 6" x 6"

BLOCKS NEEDED: 4 Road to Oklahoma blocks

Spring flowers signal the changing of the seasons in the high desert of Oregon where we live. Bright colors peeking up through the snow herald the end of winter. Warmer days are ahead, and the promise of floral pinks, greens, yellows, oranges, and magentas helps to keep our spirits soaring. *Spring Flowers* was inspired by the bright border fabric; it called to us, just begging to be turned into a quilt. A simple background and appliquéd flowers tossed on the quilt top make this a great spring project.

CUTTING

Prepare the fabric following the Essential Instructions on page 11.

Light green: Cut 4 strips $3^1/2$" wide, then cut into 38 squares $3^1/2$" x $3^1/2$" for the background.

Yellow: Cut 3 strips $3^1/2$" wide, then cut into 30 squares $3^1/2$" x $3^1/2$" for the background.

Light orange: Cut 2 strips $3^1/2$" wide, then cut into 20 squares $3^1/2$" x $3^1/2$" for the background.

Pink: Cut 2 strips $3^1/2$" wide, then cut into 20 squares $3^1/2$" x $3^1/2$" for the background.

Dark green: Cut 1 strip $2^1/2$" wide, then cut into 4 squares $2^1/2$" x $2^1/2$" for the Road to Oklahoma blocks.

Dark orange: Cut 1 strip $6^3/4$" wide. Cut into 2 rectangles $6^3/4$" x $19^1/4$", which will be cut later into the side border triangles.

Cut 1 strip $6^3/4$" wide. Cut into 2 rectangles $6^3/4$" x $14^3/4$", which will be cut later into the top and bottom border triangles.

Cut 1 strip $2^1/2$" wide, then cut into 12 squares $2^1/2$" x $2^1/2$" for the Road to Oklahoma blocks.

Cut 1 strip $2^7/8$" wide for the Road to Oklahoma blocks.

Floral print: Cut 1 strip $2^1/2$" wide, then cut into 4 squares $2^1/2$" x $2^1/2$" for the Road to Oklahoma blocks.

Cut 1 strip $2^7/8$" wide for the Road to Oklahoma blocks.

Cut 1 strip $6^3/4$" wide. Cut into 2 rectangles $6^3/4$" x $19^1/4$", which will be cut later into the side border triangles.

Cut 1 strip $6^3/4$" wide. Cut into 2 rectangles $6^3/4$" x $14^3/4$", which will be cut later into the top and bottom border triangles.

Binding: Cut 5 strips $2^1/2$" wide.

BLOCK ASSEMBLY

Refer to the Essential Instructions on page 12.

1. Refer to the Essential Instructions on page 13 to make 16 half-square triangle units using the floral print and dark orange $2^7/8$" x $2^7/8$" strips.

2. Lay out 1 dark green $2^1/2$" x $2^1/2$" square, 4 half-square triangle units, 3 orange $2^1/2$" x $2^1/2$" squares, and 1 floral print $2^1/2$" x $2^1/2$" square. Arrange as shown on the Road to Oklahoma Assembly Diagram.

3. Sew the units into rows and press. Sew the rows together and press. Make 4. Set aside.

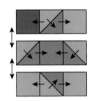

Road to Oklahoma Block Assembly, make 4.

QUILT ASSEMBLY

1. Lay out the background squares following the Quilt Assembly Diagram.

2. Refer to page 31 for piecing the side, top, and bottom triangles. Make 2 L triangle units and 2 R triangle units $6^1/2$" x 14" for the top and bottom border. Make 2 L triangle units and 2 R triangle units $6^1/2$" x $18^1/2$" for the sides. Press.

3. Sew 1 L triangle unit and 1 R triangle unit together as shown in the Quilt Assembly Diagram. Press. Make 2 side borders and 2 top and bottom borders.

4. Add a side border to each side of the quilt top. Press.

5. Referring to the Quilt Assembly Diagram for placement, sew a Road to Oklahoma Block to each end of the top and bottom triangle borders. Add the borders to the quilt top. Press.

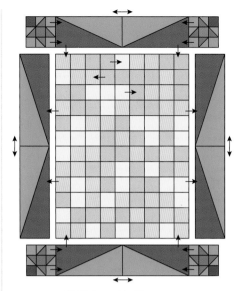

Quilt Assembly Diagram

APPLIQUÉ

Refer to the Essential Instructions on pages 15.

1. Enlarge the patterns on pages 34-35 for 4 Flowers B (3 will use alternate center), 2 Flowers C (at different sizes), 1 Flower D, 1 Flower E, 2 Flowers F (1 will use alternate center), 5 Tails A, 7 Tails A reversed, 3 Tails B, 1 Tail B reversed, 1 Tail C, and 1 Tail C reversed. Trace the enlarged patterns onto the paper side of the paper-backed fusible web. Cut the required number of shapes from each of the fabrics. Refer to the photo and patterns for flower design and placement.

2. Assemble the appliqué shapes for each flower on an appliqué pressing sheet and fuse together. Referring to the photo for flower and tail placement, position the shapes on the quilt and fuse in place.

3. Refer to page 15 for buttonhole appliqué instructions.

FINISHING

Refer to the Essential Instructions on page 17.

1. Layer the backing, batting, and quilt top; baste.
2. Quilt as desired.
3. Attach a hanging sleeve, if desired.
4. Bind or finish as desired.
5. Attach a label.

Flower D
Enlarge 200%
Make 1 for quilt.

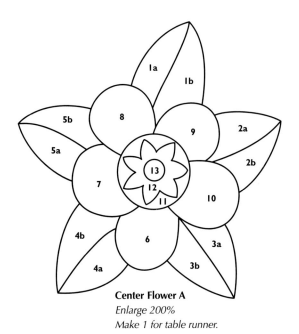

Center Flower A
Enlarge 200%
Make 1 for table runner.

Spring Flowers Quilt Appliqué Patterns

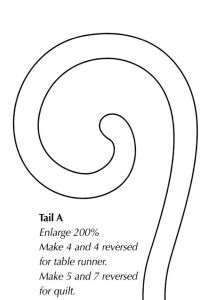

Tail A
Enlarge 200%
Make 4 and 4 reversed
for table runner.
Make 5 and 7 reversed
for quilt.

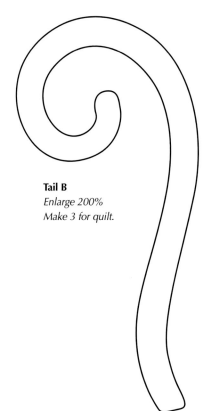

Tail B
Enlarge 200%
Make 3 for quilt.

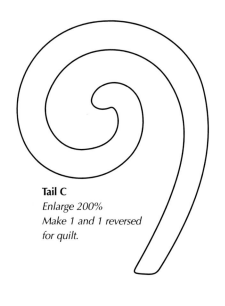

Tail C
Enlarge 200%
Make 1 and 1 reversed
for quilt.

Flower E
Enlarge 200%
Make 1 for quilt.

Flower C
Make 1 at 200%
and 1 at 275% for quilt.

Alternate Flower B Center
Enlarge 200%
Make 3 for quilt.

Alternate Flower F Center
Enlarge 200%
Make 1 for quilt.

Flower F
Enlarge 200%
Make 2 for quilt.

Flower B
Make 2 at 200%
for table runner.
Make 4 at 200%
for quilt.

April

TROPICAL DREAM MANTLE TOPPER

FINISHED PROJECT SIZE: 60" x 17"

FINISHED BLOCK SIZE: 6" x 6"

BLOCKS NEEDED: 4 small Palm blocks

This mantle topper adds a touch of the tropics to any fireplace or shelf. It also makes a great table runner. Learn how to paper piece with this fun project.

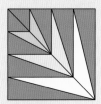

Palm Block

MATERIALS

Light gold: 1/4 yard for the Palm blocks

Medium gold: 1/4 yard for the Palm blocks

Dark gold: 1/4 yard for the Palm blocks and Border 1

Green: 1/2 yard for the Palm blocks

Red: 1/4 yard for Border 2

Blue: 3/8 yard for Border 2

Purple: 1/4 yard for Border 2

Binding: 1/2 yard

Backing: 1 yard

Batting: 4 squares 15" x 15"

Other materials: Lightweight paper for paper piecing, fine-tip permanent marker, spray starch, and 5 buttons, approx. 1" in diameter (optional)

CUTTING

Prepare the fabric according to the Essential Instructions on page 11.

Dark gold Border 1: Cut 4 strips $1^1/2$" wide, then cut into 8 strips $1^1/2$" x $6^1/2$" and 8 strips $1^1/2$" x $8^1/2$".

Blue Border 2: Cut 2 strips $2^1/2$" wide, then cut into 4 strips 2 1/2" x $8^1/2$" and 4 strips $2^1/2$" x $12^1/2$".

Purple Border 2: Cut 1 strip $2^1/2$" wide, then cut into 2 strips $2^1/2$" x $8^1/2$" and 2 strips $2^1/2$" x $12^1/2$".

Red Border 2: Cut 1 strip $2^1/2$" wide, then cut into 2 strips $2^1/2$" x $8^1/2$" and 2 strips $2^1/2$" x $12^1/2$".

Backing: Cut 4 squares 15" x 15".

Binding: Cut 5 strips 2" wide.

BLOCK ASSEMBLY

Refer to the Essential Instructions on page 14.

1. Enlarge 200% the small Palm block A and B patterns on page 41. Make 4 copies each on paper-piecing paper. Refer to the photo, diagram below, and Palm block pattern for placement of fabric, sewing order, and pressing directions. To make piecing easier, write the fabric color of each piece on paper with a fine tip marker.

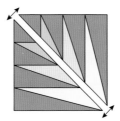

Palm Block

2. Paper piece each Palm block unit A and unit B following the numerical order on the pattern. Spray starch and press.

3. Sew unit A to unit B. Press seam open. Make 4 blocks. Remove the paper.

BORDERS

Refer to the Essential Instructions on page 16.

1. Add Border 1 to the sides and then to the top and bottom of each block. Press.

2. Add blue Border 2 to 2 of the blocks in the same manner.

3. Add red Border 2 to one side of each of the remaining blocks. Add the purple Border 2 to the opposite side of the blocks. Press.

4. Repeat, adding the remaining red and purple borders.

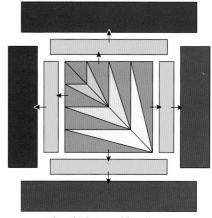

Palm Block Assembly Diagram

FINISHING

Refer to the Essential Instructions on page 17.

1. Layer the backing, batting, and block; baste.

2. Quilt each block as desired.

3. Bind each block.

4. Attach all 4 units together by stitching on buttons, sewing together without buttons, or using snaps. Add an additional button onto each end if desired.

5. Attach a label.

TIP *To make the topper drape over the edge of a mantle or shelf, press the topper in half lengthwise. If the topper will not stay on the mantle or shelf, attach a small weight to the underside top corner of each block.*

TROPICAL DREAM QUILT

Pieced by Pam Nelson

FINISHED QUILT SIZE: $64^{1}/_{2}$" x $78^{1}/_{2}$"

FINISHED BLOCK SIZES: 6" x 6" and 10" x 10"

BLOCKS NEEDED: 4 small Palm and 4 large Palm blocks

We live in a part of the country where April weather ranges from sunny and 70° to snowing and 20°. On the cold and snowy days, this project reminds us that warm weather will soon be here!

FABRIC SELECTION TIPS

Select the border print fabric first. Choose a print that has at least 5 different colors in it. Next select the light and dark red, blue, purple, and gold (or other colors that match your border fabric). Make sure both the dark and light fabrics are of similar value. Check to see if there is enough contrast between the dark and light fabrics by squinting at the fabric from a distance. The contrast should be easily distinguished. Select the medium gold. Finally, select the green fabric to coordinate with the border print fabric.

MATERIALS

Light gold: $^{1}/_{4}$ yard for the Palm blocks

Medium gold: $^{1}/_{2}$ yard for the Palm blocks and squares

Dark gold: $^{5}/_{8}$ yard for the Palm blocks, squares, and corner triangles

Green: $1^{5}/_{8}$ yards for the Palm blocks, squares, and side setting triangles

Light red: $^{3}/_{4}$ yard for the squares and Border 1

Dark red: $^{5}/_{8}$ yard for the squares and corner triangle

Light purple: $^{5}/_{8}$ yard for the squares and corner triangle

Dark purple: $^{3}/_{4}$ yard for the squares and Border 3

Light blue: $1^{1}/_{8}$ yards for the squares, Border 2, and corner triangle

Dark blue: $^{1}/_{4}$ yard for the squares

Tropical print: $1^{1}/_{2}$ yards for Border 4

Binding: $^{3}/_{4}$ yard

Backing: 5 yards

Batting: 69" x 83"

Other materials: Lightweight paper for paper piecing, fine-tip permanent marker, and spray starch

MATERIALS

Sky blue: 1 fat quarter for background

Yellow: Scrap or fat quarter for butterfly

Orange: Scrap or fat quarter for butterfly

Purple: Scrap or fat quarter for butterfly

Pink: 1/2 yard for butterfly, Border 1, and flower

Black: Scrap or fat quarter for butterfly and flower

Red: Scrap or fat quarter for flower

Medium orange: Scrap or fat quarter for flower

Dark green: Scrap or fat quarter for leaves

Light green: 1/4 yard for leaves and Border 2

Dark blue: 1/4 yard for Border 3

Backing: 1 1/8 yard

Batting: 13" x 13"; 21" x 21"

Paper-backed fusible web: 1/2 yard (12" wide)

Pillow form: 20" x 20"

Other materials: Appliqué pressing sheet, tear-away stabilizer, water-soluble thread, rayon decorative threads, fabric-marking pencil or pen, and fine-tip permanent marker

CUTTING

Prepare the fabric according to the Essential Instructions on page 11.

Sky blue: Cut 1 square 13" x 13" for pillow center; this will be trimmed after the appliqué is complete.

Pink Border 1: Cut 2 strips 1 1/2" wide, then cut into 2 strips 1 1/2" x 12 1/2" and 2 strips 1 1/2" x 14 1/2".

Light green Border 2: Cut 2 strips 1 1/2" wide, then cut into 2 strips 1 1/2" x 14 1/2" and 2 strips 1 1/2" x 16 1/2".

Dark blue Border 3: Cut 2 strips 2 1/2" wide, then cut into 2 strips 2 1/2" x 16 1/2" and 2 strips 2 1/2" x 20 1/2".

Backing: Cut 1 square 21" x 21".

Cut 1 rectangle 11" x 20 1/2" and 1 rectangle 14" x 20 1/2" for the back of the pillow.

APPLIQUÉ

Refer to the Essential Instructions on page 15.

1. Enlarge 200% and trace the Butterfly A and Butterfly Garden patterns on page 46–47 to the paper side of the paper-backed fusible web. Referring to the photo, cut the required number of shapes from each of the fabrics.

2. Assemble the appliqué shapes onto an appliqué pressing sheet, following the placement on the Butterfly Garden Pillow Pattern. Fuse the butterfly, then the flowers and leaves, together. Fuse all pieces to the blue background.

3. Refer to page 15 for decorative stitching techniques. Use decorative stitches on the butterfly, leaves, and flowers, following the pattern on the Butterfly Garden Pattern, or as desired. The edges of the fused pieces need to be secured.

4. Machine trapunto the butterfly, leaves, and flowers by placing a thin layer of cotton batting behind each piece. Stitch around the outside of each shape with the water-soluble thread in the top needle. Turn the pillow over and cut away any batting beyond the stitching line.

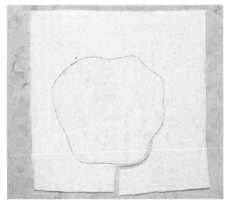

Trapunto process

5. Trim the center of the pillow to 12 1/2" x 12 1/2".

BORDERS

Refer to the Essential Instructions on page 16.

1. Sew the Border 1 side borders onto the pillow top, then add the Border 1 top and bottom borders. Press toward the borders.

2. Add Borders 2 and 3 in the same manner.

FINISHING

Refer to the Essential Instructions on pages 17.

1. Layer the 21" x 21" backing, batting, and pillow top; baste.

2. Quilt as desired, up to the edge of the trapunto stitching. Stitch sparingly in the trapuntoed area near the satin-stitched lines, but not on top of them, to secure the layers together. Remove the water-soluble thread following the manufacturer's instructions.

3. Trim to 20 1/2" x 20 1/2".

4. Make the back of the pillow using the 11" x 20 1/2" and 14" x 20 1/2" rectangles following the Essential Instructions on page 18.

5. Stuff with a 20" x 20" pillow form.

6. Label if desired.

Butterfly Garden Quilt

FINISHED QUILT SIZE: 48" x 37"

This Butterfly Garden will never need weeding. Regardless of the weather, the quilt will make any room bright and sunny. This is a fast and fun machine appliqué project.

FABRIC SELECTION TIPS

Select a clear, light blue for the sky background. Next choose the yellow for the butterfly, then the contrasting bright butterfly colors in oranges and purples. The flower colors of red, pink, and gold should be low in contrast. Choose high-contrast greens in the same color range in light, medium, and dark values for the leaves. The outer border fabric should be a dark blue tone-on-tone print.

MATERIALS

Sky blue: ³/₄ yard for background

Yellow: 1 fat quarter for butterfly

Orange print: Scraps or fat quarter for butterflies

Purple: 1 fat quarter or scraps for butterflies

Black: 1 fat quarter or scraps for butterflies and flowers

Red: ¹/₂ yard for flowers

Medium orange print: 1 fat quarter or scraps for flowers

Pink: ¹/₂ yard for flowers and Border 1

Gold: 1 fat quarter or scraps for flowers

Light green: 1 fat quarter for leaves

Medium green print: 1 fat quarter for leaves

Medium green solid: ¹/₃ yard for leaves and Border 2

Dark green: 1 fat quarter for leaves

Dark blue: ⁷/₈ yard for Border 3

Binding: ¹/₂ yard

Backing: 2 yards

Batting: 52" x 41"

Fusible web: 1¹/₂ yards (12" wide)

Other materials: Appliqué pressing sheet, tear-away stabilizer, rayon decorative threads, fabric-marking pencil or pen, and fine-tip permanent marker

CUTTING

Prepare the fabric according to the Essential Instructions on page 11.

Sky blue: Cut 1 rectangle 34" x 23"; this will be trimmed after the appliqué is complete.

Pink Border 1: Cut 4 strips 1¹/₂" wide, then cut into 2 strips 1¹/₂" x 33", and 2 strips 1¹/₂" x 24".

Green Border 2: Cut 4 strips 1¹/₂" wide, then cut into 2 strips 1¹/₂" x 35" and 2 strips 1¹/₂" x 26".

Dark blue Border 3: Cut 4 strips 6" wide, then cut into 4 strips 6" x 37".

Binding: Cut 5 strips 2¹/₂" wide.

APPLIQUÉ

Refer to the Essential Instructions on page 15.

1. Enlarge 200% and trace 1 each of Butterfly A, B, and C, 3 Flower A, 3 Flower B, and several copies of each leaf pattern on pages 46–47. You may choose to add more leaves as you build your design. Use the color photo and the instructions on page 15 to assemble, fuse, and stitch the appliqué design. The quilt is not machine trapuntoed, but may be if you choose. Refer to Appliqué, Step 4 on page 43.

2. Trim the center to 33" x 22".

BORDERS

Refer to the Essential Instructions on page 16.

1. Sew the Border 1 top and bottom borders to the quilt top, then add the Border 1 side borders. Press toward the border.

2. Add Border 2 and 3 in the same manner.

FINISHING

Refer to the Essential Instructions on page 17.

1. Layer the backing, batting, and quilt top; baste.

2. Quilt as desired.

3. Attach a hanging sleeve if desired.

4. Bind or finish as desired.

5. Attach a label.

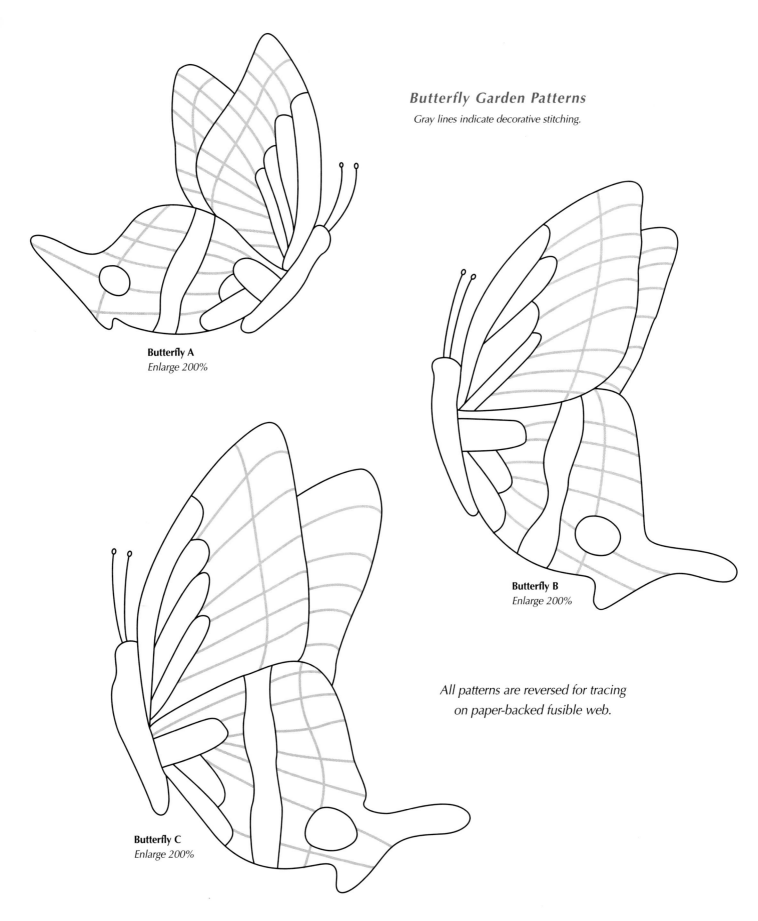

Butterfly Garden Patterns
Gray lines indicate decorative stitching.

Butterfly A
Enlarge 200%

Butterfly B
Enlarge 200%

Butterfly C
Enlarge 200%

*All patterns are reversed for tracing
on paper-backed fusible web.*

Butterfly Garden Patterns
Gray lines indicate decorative stitching.

Flower A
Enlarge 200%

Leaf
Enlarge 200%

Leaf
Enlarge 200%

Flower B
Enlarge 200%

Butterfly Garden Pattern
Enlarge 200%

Leaf
Enlarge 200%

Leaf
Enlarge 200%

Leaf
Enlarge 200%

June

Technique: Strip Piecing and Paper Piecing

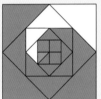 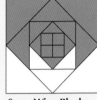

Swan Head Block   **Swan Wing Block**

 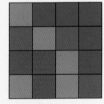

Wave Block   **16-Patch Block**

SERENITY WALLHANGING

FINISHED PROJECT SIZE: 31³/₄" x 31³/₄"

FINISHED BLOCK SIZES: 8" x 8"

BLOCKS NEEDED: 1 Swan Head block, 1 Swan Wing block, 3 Wave blocks (2 will be cut in half), and 3 16-Patch blocks (1 will be cut in half)

We just can't resist the beauty of the serene lakes, mountains, and swans that surround us in Oregon. They sneak into many of our designs. This project involves some strip piecing and more advanced paper-piecing techniques. Careful color selection and placement are essential to the success of this quilt. Look through your stash or a quilting friend's scrap basket; you'll most likely discover most of the fabrics needed to make this project.

MATERIALS

Light blue: ¹/₂ yard for the Swan Head, Swan Wing, and Wave blocks, and setting triangles

Medium blue: ³/₈ yard for the 16-Patch block and Wave blocks

Green small print: Large scrap or fat quarter for the 16-Patch block

Green medium print: Large scrap or fat quarter for the 16-Patch block

Green/brown multicolored print: ¹/₂ yard for the 16-Patch block and setting triangles

Orange: 2¹/₂" x 2¹/₂" scrap for the Swan Head block

Off-white: ¹/₄ yard or fat quarter for the Swan Head, Swan Wing, and Wave blocks

Purple: ¼ yard for inner border

Black: ⅝ yard for outer border

Binding: ⅜ yard

Backing: 1 yard

Batting: 36" x 36"

Other materials: Paper-piecing paper, fine-tip permanent marker, and spray starch

CUTTING

Prepare the fabric according to the Essential Instructions on page 11. Note: The rotary cutting directions for some of the setting triangles call for cutting a square, then cutting the square into 4 triangles. This may waste some fabric so you may want to create a template using the sizes shown to cut just the number of triangles you need.

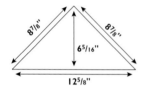

Light blue: Cut 1 square 12⅝" x 12⅝", then cut twice diagonally for the side setting triangle.

Cut 1 square 6½" x 6½", then cut in half diagonally for the top corner setting triangles.

Cut 1 square 2⅜" x 2⅜", then cut in half diagonally for the Swan Head block.

Cut 7 squares 2" x 2" for the Swan Head and Wing blocks.

Medium blue: Cut 9 squares 2½" x 2½" for the 16-Patch blocks.

Green small print: Cut 9 squares 2½" x 2½" for the 16-Patch blocks.

Green medium print: Cut 8 squares 2½" x 2½" for the 16-Patch blocks.

Green/brown multicolored print: Cut 1 square 6½" x 6½", then cut in half diagonally for the bottom corner setting triangles.

Cut 16 squares 2½" x 2½" for the 16-Patch blocks.

Orange: Cut 1 square 2⅜" x 2⅜", then cut in half diagonally for the Swan Head block.

Purple inner border: Cut 4 strips 1½" wide, then cut into 2 strips 1½" x 25¼" and 2 strips 1½" x 23¼".

Black outer border: Cut 4 strips 4" wide, then cut into 2 strips 4" x 32¼" and 2 strips 4" x 25¼".

Binding: Cut 4 strips 2½" wide.

BLOCK ASSEMBLY

Refer to the Essential Instructions on page 14.

1. Enlarge 200% the Swan Head, Swan Wing, and Wave block patterns on pages 53–54. Make 1 copy each of the Swan Head and Swan Wing patterns, and 3 of the Wave patterns, on paper-piecing paper. To make piecing easier, refer to the Wallhanging Assembly Diagram, and write the fabric color of each piece on the paper with a fine-tip permanent marker. Remember, the paper piecing patterns are mirror imaged, so mark the paper-piecing patterns accordingly.

2. To make the Swan Head block, you will sew the center together before paper piecing. Sew 1 light blue triangle to an orange triangle. Press. Sew 3 blue 2" x 2" squares and the triangle unit together as shown. Press. This pieced unit is larger than needed for the center of the Swan Head block and will be trimmed during paper piecing.

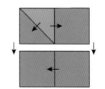

Center of Swan Head Block

3. Paper piece the Swan Head block following the numerical order on the pattern. Match the seams of the pieced center unit with the lines on the center (1) of the block, and pin to the paper pattern. Treat this center unit as Piece 1 and continue to paper piece the rest of the block.

4. To make the Swan Wing block, sew 4 blue 2" x 2" squares together before paper piecing. Press.

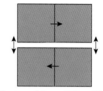

Center of Swan Wing Block

5. Paper piece the Swan Wing block in the same manner as the Swan Head block.

6. Paper piece the Wave block units separately following the numerical order on the pattern. Refer to the Wallhanging Assembly Diagram for the color placement in the blocks, making special note of the color placement in the side Wave blocks.

7. Sew Wave block units B, C, and D together. Press. Add units A and E. Press.

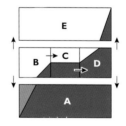

Wave Block Assembly Diagram

8. Trim the 2 side Wave blocks. Be sure to leave a 1/4" seam allowance beyond the stitching line.

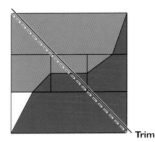

Trim for the right side setting Wave block.

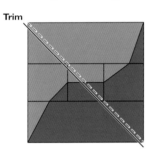

Trim for the left side setting Wave block.

9. Sew the 16-Patch blocks together. Refer to the Wallhanging Assembly Diagram and photo for color placement. Sew the squares together into rows and press. Sew the rows together to create the block. Press.

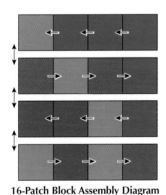

16-Patch Block Assembly Diagram

10. Sew the 16-Patch bottom setting triangle block together using 10 squares as shown. Press. Trim, being sure to leave a 1/4" seam allowance beyond the stitching line.

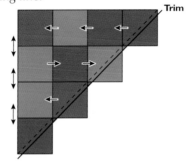

16-Patch Bottom Setting Triangle Block

WALLHANGING ASSEMBLY

1. Lay out all of the blocks as shown in the Wallhanging Assembly Diagram.
2. Pin and sew the blocks into rows. Press.
3. Pin, then sew the rows together. Press.

BORDERS

Refer to the Essential Instructions on page 16.

1. Sew the inner border to the sides, then to the top and bottom of the quilt top. Press.
2. Add the outside border in the same manner.

FINISHING

Refer to the Essential instructions on page 17.

1. Layer the backing, batting, and quilt top; baste.
2. Quilt as desired.
3. Attach a hanging sleeve if desired.
4. Bind or finish as desired.
5. Attach a label.

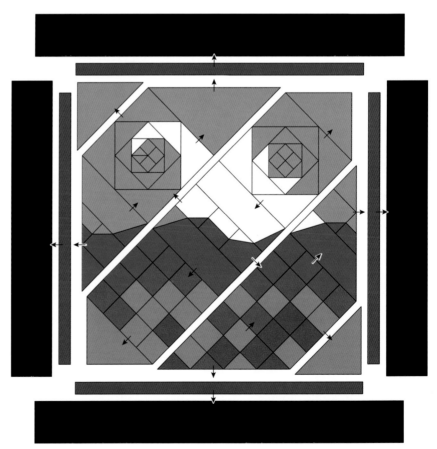

Wallhanging Assembly Diagram

Serenity Quilt

Pieced by Virginia Mohr

FINISHED QUILT SIZE: 70" x 81³/₈"

FINISHED BLOCK SIZE: 8" x 8"

BLOCKS NEEDED: 7 Swan Head and 4 Swan Wing blocks, 15 Wave blocks, 12 16-Patch blocks, 6 16-Patch Side and Corner Setting Triangle blocks

This quilt was inspired by an annual festival that celebrates the city park and its swans. The festival was revived a few years ago, and one of its main features is a giant floating swan on Mirror Pond. Mountains to the west provide the perfect backdrop for this serene setting. The quilt is not difficult to piece, but you should pay attention to the color arrangement in the Assembly Diagram on page 53. It helps to arrange the blocks on a design wall as you sew.

FABRIC SELECTION TIPS

Bali fabrics work well for this quilt. A light blue for the sky should be the easiest fabric to find. The 3 water fabrics should be similar in value, but different enough so the waves are obvious. Choose small, medium, and multicolored green prints similar in value to the blues you selected for the water, and one dark green print. Select a medium and a slightly darker purple for the mountain. Look for a blue-black for the outer border. The swans are black and off-white.

MATERIALS

Light blue: ⁵/₈ yard for the 16-Patch blocks and triangles

Medium purple: ⁵/₈ yard for the 16-Patch blocks and triangle

Dark purple: ⁵/₈ yard for the 16-Patch blocks and inner border

Green/brown multicolored print: 1 yard for the 16-Patch blocks, squares, and triangles

Green small print: ³/₈ yard for the 16-Patch blocks

Green medium print: ¹/₄ yard for the 16-Patch blocks

Dark green print: ¹/₃ yard for the 16-Patch blocks

Blue print: 1¹/₂ yards for the 16-Patch, Swan Head, Swan Wing, and Wave blocks, squares, and triangles

Blue multicolored print: 1 yard for the squares, and triangles

Blue solid: 1 yard for the Swan Head, Swan Wing and Wave blocks, squares, and triangles

Black fabric: 1⁷/₈ yards for the Swan Head, Swan Wing, and Wave blocks, and outer border

Off-white: ⁷/₈ yard for the Swan Head, Swan Wing, and Wave blocks

Orange: Large scrap or fat quarter for the Swan Head blocks

Backing: 5 yards

Batting: 74" x 85"

Binding: $^3/_4$ yard

Other materials: Lightweight paper for paper-piecing, fine-tip permanent marker, and spray starch

CUTTING

Prepare the fabric according to the Essential Instructions on page 11. Note: The rotary cutting directions for some of the setting triangles call for cutting a square, then cutting the square into 4 triangles. This may waste some fabric so you may want to create a template using the sizes shown on page 49 to cut just the number of triangles you need.

Light blue: Cut 1 square 12$^5/_8$" x 12$^5/_8$", then cut twice diagonally for the side setting triangles.

Cut 1 square 6$^1/_2$" x 6$^1/_2$", then cut in half diagonally for the top corner triangles.

Cut 2 strips 2$^1/_2$" wide, then cut into 28 squares 2$^1/_2$" x 2$^1/_2$" for the 16-Patch blocks.

Medium purple: Cut 1 square 12$^5/_8$" x 12$^5/_8$", then cut twice diagonally for a side setting triangle.

Cut 2 strips 2$^1/_2$" wide, then cut into 23 squares 2$^1/_2$" x 2$^1/_2$" for the 16-Patch blocks.

Dark purple: Cut 2 strips 2$^1/_2$" wide, then cut into 32 squares 2$^1/_2$" x 2$^1/_2$" for the 16-Patch blocks.

Inner border: Cut 7 strips 1$^1/_2$". Sew into one long strip, then cut into 2 strips 1$^1/_2$" x 59", and 2 strips 1$^1/_2$" x 68$^3/_8$".

Green/brown multicolored print:

Cut 1 square 12$^5/_8$" x 12$^5/_8$", then cut twice diagonally for a side setting triangle.

Cut 3 squares 8$^1/_2$" x 8$^1/_2$".

Cut 3 strips 2$^1/_2$" wide, then cut into 43 squares 2$^1/_2$" x 2$^1/_2$" for the 16-Patch blocks.

Green small print: Cut 3 strips 2$^1/_2$" x 2$^1/_2$", then cut into 41 squares 2$^1/_2$" x 2$^1/_2$" for the 16-Patch blocks.

Green medium print: Cut 1 strip 2$^1/_2$" wide, then cut into 17 squares 2$^1/_2$" x 2$^1/_2$" for the 16-Patch blocks.

Dark green print: Cut 3 strips 2$^1/_2$" wide, then cut into 37 squares 2$^1/_2$" x 2$^1/_2$" for the 16-Patch blocks.

Blue print: Cut 1 square 12$^5/_8$" x 12$^5/_8$", then cut twice diagonally for the side setting triangles.

Cut 6 squares 8$^1/_2$" x 8$^1/_2$".

Cut 2 strips 2$^1/_2$" wide, then cut into 24 squares 2$^1/_2$" x 2$^1/_2$" for the 16-Patch blocks.

Blue multicolored print: Cut 1 square 12$^5/_8$" x 12$^5/_8$", then cut twice diagonally for the side setting triangles.

Cut 2 squares 8$^1/_2$" x 8$^1/_2$".

Blue solid: Cut 1 square 12$^5/_8$" x 12$^5/_8$", then cut twice diagonally for the side setting triangles.

Cut 1 square 8$^1/_2$" x 8 $^1/_2$".

Black outer border: Cut 8 strips 6" wide. Sew into one long strip, then cut into 2 strips 6" x 70$^3/_8$" and 2 strips 6" x 70".

Binding: Cut 9 strips 2$^1/_2$" wide.

BLOCK ASSEMBLY

Refer to the Essential Instructions on page 14. Place all the finished blocks on the design wall in the correct location, adjusting the color of the blocks if necessary.

1. Refer to page 49 to paper piece 7 Swan Head and 4 Wing blocks.

2. Refer to page 49 to paper piece the 15 Wave blocks. Refer to the Quilt Assembly Diagram and photo for color placement.

3. Refer to page 50 to make 12 of the 16-Patch blocks. Refer to the Quilt Assembly Diagram and photo for color placement.

4. Refer to page 50 to make 4 of the 16-Patch side setting triangle blocks.

5. Sew 2 bottom corner triangle blocks using 6 squares as shown. Press. Trim, being sure to leave a $^1/_4$" seam allowance beyond the stitching line.

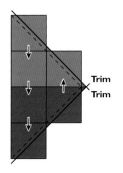

Bottom Corner Triangle Block Assembly Diagram

QUILT ASSEMBLY

1. Lay out all of the blocks as shown in the Quilt Assembly Diagram.

2. This quilt is diagonally set. Careful sewing and alignment is essential. Pin and sew the blocks into rows as indicated on the Quilt Assembly Diagram, carefully matching seams. Note: Press all seams open.

BORDERS

Refer to the Essential Instructions on page 16.

1. Add the purple inner side borders, then the top and bottom borders. Press.

2. Add the black outer side borders in the same manner.

FINISHING

Refer to the Essential Instructions on page 17.

1. Layer the backing, batting, and quilt top; baste.
2. Quilt as desired.
3. Attach a hanging sleeve, if desired.
4. Bind or finish as desired.
5. Attach a label.

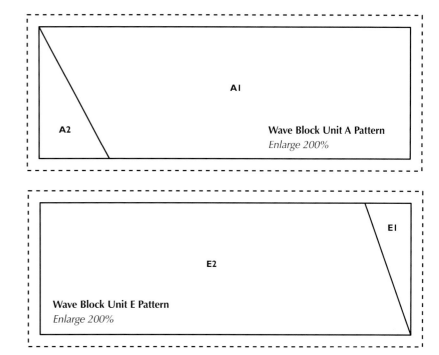

A1

A2

Wave Block Unit A Pattern
Enlarge 200%

E1

E2

Wave Block Unit E Pattern
Enlarge 200%

Serenity Quilt Patterns

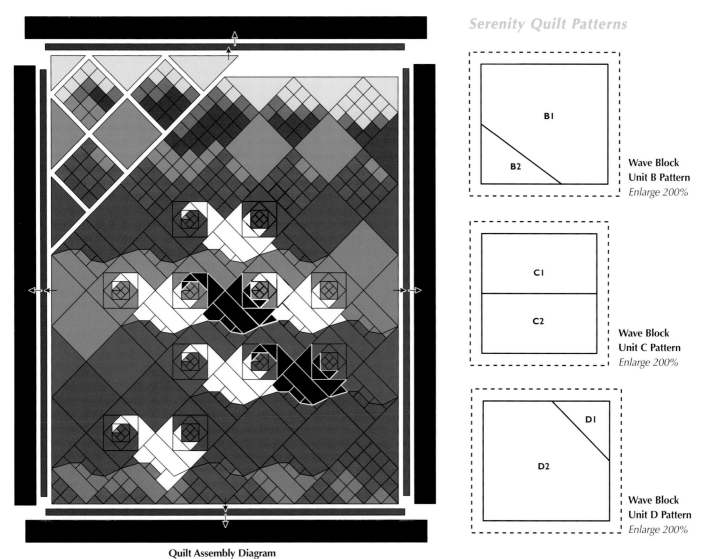

Quilt Assembly Diagram

B1

B2

Wave Block Unit B Pattern
Enlarge 200%

C1

C2

Wave Block Unit C Pattern
Enlarge 200%

D1

D2

Wave Block Unit D Pattern
Enlarge 200%

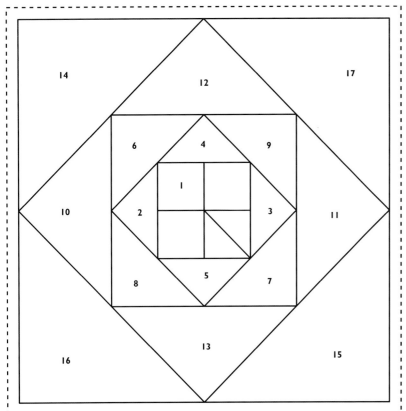

Swan Head Block Pattern
Enlarge 200%

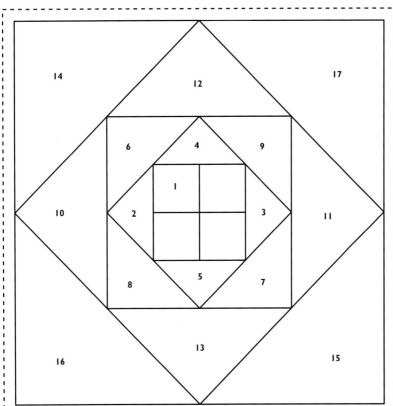

Swan Wing Block Pattern
Enlarge 200%

Spinner Block

MATERIALS

Red: 3/4 yard for the Spinner blocks

Orange: 1 yard for the Spinner blocks and inner border

Dark blue: 1³/4 yards for the Spinner blocks and triangles

Fireworks print: 2 yards for the Spinner blocks and outer border

Binding: 3/4 yard

Backing: 3³/4 yards

Batting: 62" x 76"

Other materials: Semi-transparent or transparent template plastic and fine-tip permanent marker

CUTTING

Prepare the fabric according to the Essential Instructions on page 11.

Red: Cut 8 strips 2¹/2" wide, then cut 4 of the strips into 16 strips 2¹/2" x 9¹/2" for the blocks.

Orange: Cut 4 strips 4¹/2" wide for the blocks.

Inner border: Cut 6 strips 1¹/2" wide. Sew into one long strip, then cut into 2 strips 1¹/2" x 57" and 2 strips 1¹/2" x 45".

Dark blue: Cut 2 strips 4³/4" wide, then cut into 8 rectangles 4³/4" x 7¹/4".

Cut these in half diagonally to make 16 triangles.

Cut

Cut on the right side of the fabric only.

Cut 3 strips 4¹/2" wide, then cut into 16 rectangles 4¹/2" x 6¹/2" for the blocks.

Cut 1 strip 4¹/2" wide, then cut into 8 squares 4¹/2" x 4¹/2" for the blocks.

Cut 2 squares 16¹/4" x 16¹/4", then cut in half diagonally to make 4 triangles for the corners.

Enlarge 200% the Celebration Corner C1 and C2 patterns on page 61 and make templates from plastic template material. Cut 2 C1 and C2 pieces. Turn the templates over and cut 2 mirror image C1 and C2 pieces.

Fireworks print: Cut 2 strips 6⁷/8" wide. Cut the strips into 8 squares 6⁷/8" x 6⁷/8", then cut in half diagonally into 16 triangles for the blocks.

Cut 2 strips 4¹/2" wide, then cut into 16 squares 4¹/2" x 4¹/2" for the blocks and corner blocks.

Outer border: Cut 6 strips 7" wide. Sew into one long strip, then cut into 2 strips 7" x 59" and 2 strips 7" x 58".

Binding: Cut 8 strips 2¹/2" wide.

BLOCK ASSEMBLY

1. Refer to page 56 to make 8 Spinner blocks.

2. Make 8 more Spinner blocks, using the blue 4¹/2" x 4¹/2" squares rather than the fireworks print.

3. Trim 2 of the blocks from Step 2 as shown to make Half Spinner blocks. Be sure to trim ¹/4" beyond the seamline.

Trim

Half Spinner Block Assembly Diagram

4. For each corner block, sew 2 fireworks print 4¹/2" x 4¹/2" squares together. Press. Sew a C1 and a C2 piece onto the sides of 2 of the square units and a C1R and a C2R piece onto the sides of the remaining square units. Press.

5. Place a pin at the center of the long edge of a 16¹/4" triangle; also place a pin in the center of a corner unit. Match the pins, then pin together, working in each direction from the center out. Sew a triangle onto each corner unit. Press.

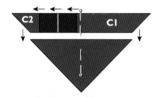

Corner Block Assembly Diagram, make 2.

Reverse Corner Block Assembly Diagram, make 2.

QUILT ASSEMBLY

1. Lay out all of the blocks as shown in the Quilt Assembly Diagram.

2. This quilt is diagonally set. Careful attention to sewing and alignment is essential. Sew 4 Spinner blocks together, paying close attention to the location of the blue and fireworks print 4" squares. Press seams open.

3. Add the corner triangle blocks. Match and pin the seams of the fireworks squares, then pin in each direction from the center out. Sew. Press.

BORDERS

Refer to the Essential Instructions page 16 .

1. Add the orange inner side borders, then the top and bottom borders. Press.

2. Add the fireworks print outer borders in the same manner.

FINISHING

Refer to the Essential Instructions on page 17.

1. Layer the backing, batting, and quilt top; baste.

2. Quilt as desired.

3. Attach a hanging sleeve if desired.

4. Bind or finish as desired.

5. Attach a label.

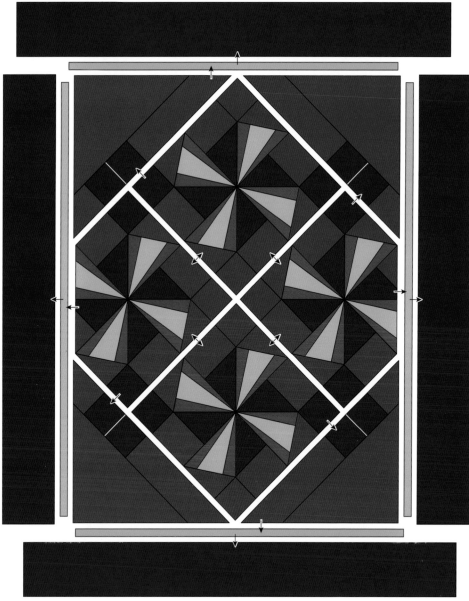

Quilt Assembly Diagram

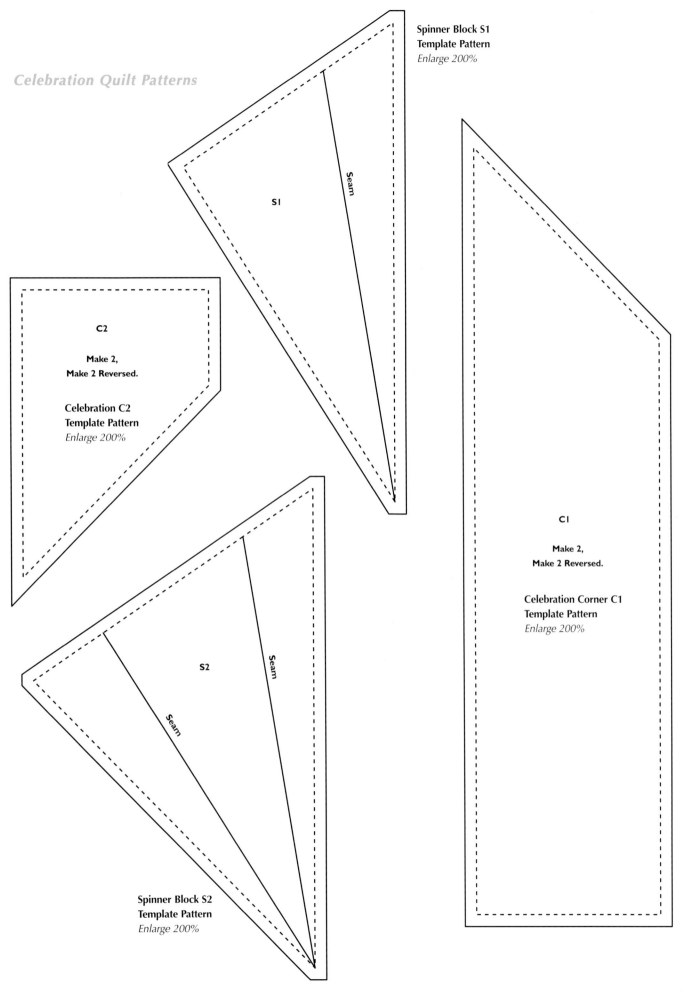

Celebration Quilt Patterns

Spinner Block S1
Template Pattern
Enlarge 200%

Seam

S1

C2

Make 2,
Make 2 Reversed.

Celebration C2
Template Pattern
Enlarge 200%

C1

Make 2,
Make 2 Reversed.

Celebration Corner C1
Template Pattern
Enlarge 200%

S2

Seam

Seam

Spinner Block S2
Template Pattern
Enlarge 200%

August

SUMMER HARVEST WALLHANGING

FINISHED PROJECT SIZE: 20" x 26"

Reminiscent of an abundant harvest, this pear wallhanging will add grace to any family gathering place. Simple Seminole piecing and hand appliqué make this a great take-along project.

MATERIALS

Beige: 1 fat quarter or $1/4$ yard for center background

Purple: $1/4$ yard for Border 1

Blue: $1/4$ yard for Border 2

Gold: $1/4$ yard for the Seminole-pieced border

Dark green: $1/2$ yard for leaves and the Seminole-pieced border

Appliqué fabrics: Fat quarters or scraps of yellow for the pears, light green for the leaves, and brown for the stems

Binding: $1/4$ yard

Backing: $2/3$ yard

Batting: 24" x 30"

Other materials: Marking pencil, freezer paper, spray starch, brown embroidery floss, and thread to match appliqué pieces

CUTTING

Prepare the fabric according to the Essential Instructions on page 11.

Beige: Cut 1 rectangle 8" x 14$1/2$".

Purple Border 1: Cut 2 strips 1$1/2$" wide, then cut into 2 strips 1$1/2$" x 8" and 2 strips 1$1/2$" x 16$1/2$".

Blue Border 2: Cut 2 strips 2" wide, then cut into 2 strips 2" x 10" and 2 strips 2" x 19".

Gold: Cut 2 strips 3" wide for the Seminole-pieced border. Cut 1 strip into 1 strip 3" x 10".

Dark green: Cut 4 strips 3" wide for the Seminole-pieced border. Cut 2 of the strips into 2 strips 3" x 10" and 8 squares 3" x 3".

Cut 1 strip 4" wide, then cut into 4 rectangles 4" x 1$^{1}/_{2}$" and 4 rectangles 4" x 4$^{1}/_{2}$".

Binding: Cut 3 strips 2$^{1}/_{2}$" wide.

CENTER ASSEMBLY

1. Add Border 1 strips to the sides, then to the top and bottom of the beige background piece. Press.

2. Add Border 2 in the same manner.

SEMINOLE-PIECED BORDER

Refer to the Essential Instructions on pages 12.

1. Sew a dark green 3"-wide strip to each side of the gold 3"-wide strip. Press. Repeat with the 3" x 10" strips to make 2 strip sets. Cut the strips into 3"-wide segments. Cut 16 segments.

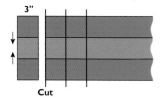

Strip piece 2 strip sets, cut 16 segments.

2. Staggering the segments as shown, sew 5 segments together for the top and bottom borders. Add 1 green 3" x 3" square to each end of the border strip as shown. Press seams in one direction. Spray starch.

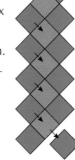

Seminole-Pieced Top and Bottom Borders, make 2.

3. Make 2 side borders in the same manner as the top and bottom borders. Sew 3 segments together. Add 1 green 3" x 3" square to each end of the border strip as shown. Press seams in one direction. Spray starch.

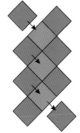

Seminole-Pieced Side Borders, make 2.

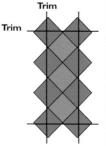

4. Trim the edges of the border strips as shown. Leave a $^{1}/_{4}$"-wide seam allowance beyond the points at each edge. Spray starch.

Trim strips, leaving $^{1}/_{4}$" seam allowance

5. Add a 1$^{1}/_{2}$" x 4" green strip to each end of the side border segments. Press.

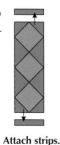

Attach strips.

6. Add a green 4$^{1}/_{2}$" x 4" rectangle to each end of the top and bottom border segments. Press.

7. Add the side border segments to the quilt center, then add the top and bottom segments. Press.

APPLIQUÉ

The appliqué shapes are sewn onto the quilt top using the needle-turn method. Refer to the Essential Instructions on pages 14.

1. Enlarge 200%, copy, and connect the Summer Harvest Appliqué layout patterns A, B, and C on page 66. Using a pencil, lightly trace the appliqué pattern layout onto the background fabric for placement of pieces.

2. Trace Summer Harvest appliqué patterns 1 to 54 onto freezer paper. Cut the required number of shapes from each of the fabrics.

3. Appliqué the pieces to the quilt top. Extend the branch and leaves into the border to complete the piece.

4. Use a stem stitch with 3 strands of brown embroidery floss for the leaf stems.

Stem stitch

FINISHING

Refer to the Essential Instructions on page 17.

1. Layer the backing, batting, and quilt top, baste.

2. Quilt as desired.

3. Attach a hanging sleeve, if desired.

4. Bind or finish as desired.

5. Attach a label.

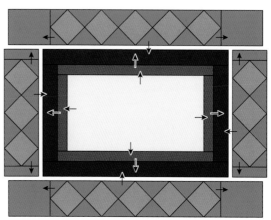

Wallhanging Assembly Diagram

Summer Harvest Quilt

Pieced by Pam Nelson

FINISHED QUILT SIZE: 38³/₄" x 38³/₄"

FINISHED BLOCK SIZE: 3¹/₂" x 3¹/₂"

BLOCKS NEEDED: 16 Square-in-a-Square blocks

Let this beautiful quilt grace your table with the colors of summer. Gold, green, purple, and blue remind us of a bountiful harvest. Simple squares pieced together to make the center and a Square-in-a-Square border finish off this quilt in record time.

FABRIC SELECTION TIPS

This quilt features 2 lights, 4 mediums, and 1 dark fabric. Choose fabrics with multiple colors that blend together to add sparkle to the quilt. Look for a dark-to-medium value green first, then select your purple and gold. Try to find a purple with some blue in it, and a gold with a bit of pink. Then pick your neutrals, and finally your dark blue to set off the quilt.

Square-in-a-Square Block

MATERIALS

Green: 1 yard for center squares, Square-in-a-Square blocks, and pieced border

Gold: ¹/₂ yard for center squares, Square-in-a-Square blocks, and corner blocks

Curry: 1 fat quarter for center squares

Purple: 1 fat quarter for center squares

Medium cream: ²/₃ yard for center squares, corner blocks, and half-square triangles

Light cream: ¹/₄ yard for the center squares and half-square triangles

Dark blue: ¹/₂ yard for half-square triangles and border

Binding: ¹/₂ yard

Backing: 1¹/₄ yards

Batting: 43" x 43"

Spray starch

CUTTING

Prepare the fabric according to the Essential Instructions on page 11.

Green: Cut 2 strips 3" wide, then cut into 15 squares 3" x 3" for the quilt center.

 Pieced border: Cut 2 strips 4" wide, then cut into 2 strips 4" x 10³/₄" and 2 strips 4" x 17³/₄".

 Pieced border: Cut 8 squares 4" x 4".

 Cut 3 strips 2⁵/₈" wide, then cut into 32 squares 2⁵/₈" x 2⁵/₈". Cut the squares diagonally to make 64 triangles for the Square-in-a-Square blocks.

Gold: Cut 3 strips 3" wide, then cut into 32 squares 3" x 3" for the center and Square-in-a-Square blocks.

 Cut 1 strip 4" wide, then cut into 4 squares 4" x 4" for the corner units.

Curry: Cut 1 strip 3" wide, then cut into 8 squares 3" x 3" for the center.

Purple: Cut 2 strips 3" wide, then cut into 16 squares 3" x 3" for the center.

Medium cream: Cut 2 strips 3" wide, then cut into 22 squares 3" x 3" for the center.

Cut 1 strip $4^3/8$" wide, then cut into 4 squares $4^3/8$" x $4^3/8$". Cut the squares diagonally to make 8 triangles for the corner blocks.

Cut 1 strip $3^3/8$" wide, then cut into 10 squares $3^3/8$" x $3^3/8$". Cut 4 squares diagonally to make 8 triangles for the center. Set aside 6 squares for 12 half-square triangles.

Light cream: Cut 1 strip 3" wide, then cut into 11 squares 3" x 3" for the center.

Cut 1 strip $3^3/8$" wide, then cut 2 squares $3^3/8$" x $3^3/8$" for 4 half-square triangles for the center.

Dark blue: Border 1: Cut 4 strips 2" wide, then cut into 2 strips 2" x $28^3/4$" and 2 strips 2" x $31^3/4$".

Cut 1 strip $3^3/8$" wide, then cut into 8 squares $3^3/8$" x $3^3/8$" for 16 half-square triangles for the center.

Cut 1 strip $3^3/8$" wide, then cut into 4 squares $3^3/8$" x $3^3/8$". Cut the squares diagonally for 8 triangles for the center.

Binding: Cut 5 strips $2^1/2$" wide.

HALF-SQUARE TRIANGLE UNITS ASSEMBLY

Refer to the Essential Instructions on page 13.

1. Make 4 light cream and dark blue half-square triangle units. These should measure 3" x 3". Press. Set aside.

2. Make 12 medium cream and dark blue half-square triangle units. These should measure 3" x 3". Press. Set aside.

Make 4.   **Make 12.**

Half-square triangle units

CORNER BLOCK ASSEMBLY

Sew 2 medium cream triangles to a gold 4" x 4" square. Spray starch. Press. Make 4 corner blocks. Set aside.

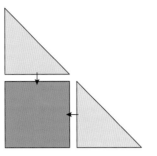

Corner Blocks, make 4.

SQUARE-IN-A-SQUARE BLOCK ASSEMBLY

1. Sew 2 green triangles to opposite sides of a gold 3" x 3" square. Press.

2. Sew 2 green triangles to the remaining sides of the gold square. Press. Make 16.

Square-in-a-Square, make 16.

☒ TIP *Fold the gold square in half and crease the center. Fold the green triangle in half and crease the center. Match the center creases and pin in place. Add the triangle and trim the dog ears.*

QUILT ASSEMBLY

1. Lay out all your blocks as shown in the Quilt Assembly Diagram.

2. Sew squares and half-square triangles together into units. Take care not to stretch the bias edges on the outside triangles. Spray starch and press.

3. Row 1: Sew Units 1 and 3 to the sides of Unit 2. Match seams and pin for accuracy. Press.

4. Row 2: Sew Units 4 and 6 to the sides of Unit 5. Press.

5. Row 3: Sew Units 7 and 9 to the sides of Unit 8. Press.

6. Sew the rows together. Press.

7. Add the Corner Triangle blocks. Press.

8. Add Border 1 to the sides, then the top and bottom borders. Press all seams toward the border. Set aside.

PIECED BORDERS

Refer to the Essential Instructions on page 16.

1. Sew a Square-in-a-Square block to each side of a green 4" x 4" square. Press. Make 8 units.

2. Sew a Square-in-a-Square unit to the sides of a green 4" x $10^3/4$" rectangle to make each side border. Press. Make 2.

3. Sew a Square-in-a-Square unit to the sides of a green 4" x $17^3/4$" rectangle to make each top and bottom border. Press. Make 2.

4. Add the borders to the sides, then the top and bottom of the quilt top. Press.

FINISHING

Refer to the Essential Instructions on page 17.

1. Layer the backing, batting, and quilt top; baste.

2. Quilt as desired.

3. Attach a hanging sleeve, if desired.

4. Bind or finish as desired.

5. Attach a label.

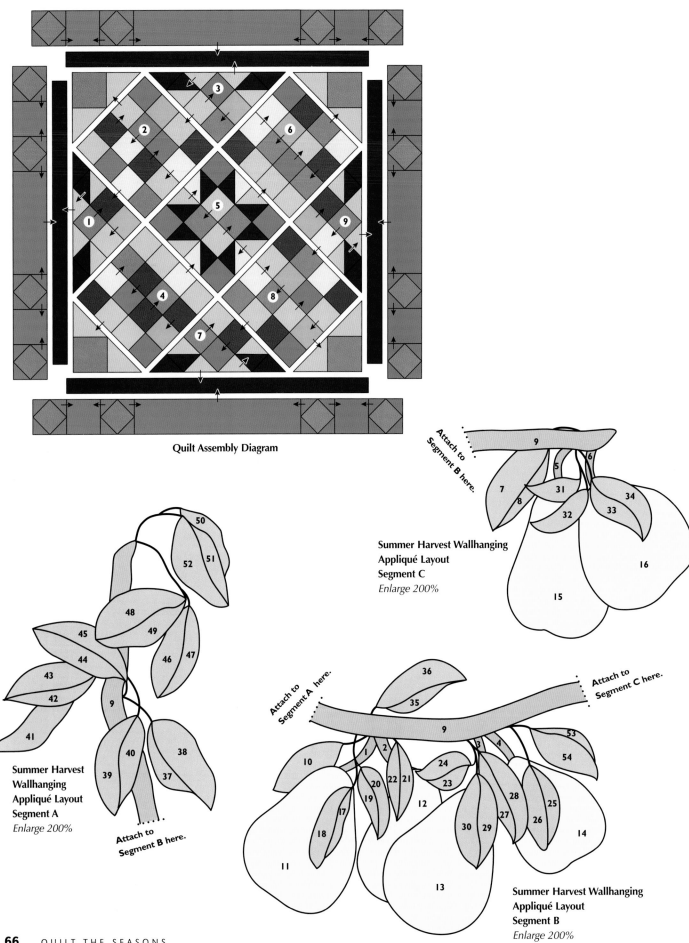

Quilt Assembly Diagram

Summer Harvest Wallhanging
Appliqué Layout
Segment C
Enlarge 200%

Summer Harvest
Wallhanging
Appliqué Layout
Segment A
Enlarge 200%

Attach to
Segment B here.

Attach to
Segment B here.

Attach to
Segment A here.

Attach to
Segment C here.

Summer Harvest Wallhanging
Appliqué Layout
Segment B
Enlarge 200%

Border 1: Cut 5 strips 2¹/₂" wide. Sew into one long strip, then cut into 2 strips 2¹/₂" x 51¹/₂" and 2 strips 2¹/₂" x 38¹/₂".

Dark blue: Cut 2 strips 1³/₄" wide for the side, top, bottom, and corner blocks.

Cut 4 strips 2" wide for the Woven Log blocks.

Border 3: Cut 6 strips 2¹/₂" wide. Sew into one long strip, then cut into 2 strips 2¹/₂" x 63¹/₂" and 2 strips 2¹/₂" x 50¹/₂".

Cut 2 squares 2¹/₂" x 2¹/₂" for the Woven Log centers.

Cut 1 strip 2⁷/₈" wide, then cut into 4 squares 2⁷/₈" x 2⁷/₈" for the side, top, bottom, and corner blocks.

Gold: Cut 12 strips 2" wide for the Woven Log blocks.

Leaf print: Cut 12 strips 3" wide for the Woven Log blocks.

Border 2: Cut 6 strips 4¹/₂" wide. Sew into one long strip, then cut into 2 strips 4¹/₂" x 55¹/₂" and 2 strips 4¹/₂" x 46¹/₂".

Binding: Cut 7 strips 2¹/₂" wide.

BLOCK ASSEMBLY

Refer to the Essential Instructions on page 12.

1. Refer to page 68 to make 8 Woven Log blocks, 2 with dark blue centers and 6 with royal blue centers. Set aside.

2. Use the same assembly method to make the side, top, and bottom blocks. Use the 13¹/₄" x 13¹/₄" square of foundation fabric, the 2⁷/₈" x 2⁷/₈" square of dark blue for the centers, and the 1³/₄"-wide strips of dark and royal blue for the strip sets. Make 3 blocks. Trim each block to 12⁷/₈" x 12⁷/₈".

3. Draw a diagonal chalk line across the block as shown. Stitch ¹/₈" on both sides of the chalk line to stabilize the fabric. Cut the block in half using the chalk line as a guide. Cut 2 blocks.

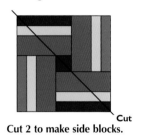
Cut 2 to make side blocks.

4. Rotate the block as shown. Draw a diagonal chalk line across the top and bottom block. Stitch ¹/₈" on both sides of the chalk line. Cut the block in half using the chalk line as a guide. Cut 1 block.

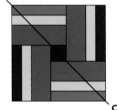
Cut 1 to make top and bottom blocks.

5. Use the same assembly method to make the corner blocks with the 13³/₄" x 13³/₄" square of foundation fabric, the dark blue 2⁷/₈" x 2⁷/₈" square for the center, and the 1³/₄"-wide strip of dark and royal blue for the strip sets. Cut strip sets 8¹/₂" long. Make 1 block. Trim to 13¹/₄" x 13¹/₄".

6. Draw 2 diagonal chalk lines across the block. Stitch ¹/₈" on each side of the chalk lines. Cut the block into 4 triangles using the chalk lines as a guide. These are the 4 corner blocks. Set aside.

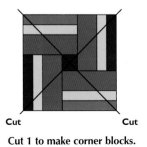
Cut 1 to make corner blocks.

QUILT ASSEMBLY

1. Lay out the blocks following the Quilt Assembly Diagram. Pay close attention to the color placement of the blocks. The rows are sewn diagonally together.

2. Sew the blocks in each row together, then sew the rows together. Press seams open.

3. Add the corner blocks. Press seams open.

BORDERS

Refer to the Essential Instructions on page 16.

1. Sew the Border 1 side strips, then the top and bottom strips to the quilt top. Press.

2. Add Borders 2 and 3 in the same manner.

FINISHING

Refer to the Essential Instructions on page 17.

1. Layer the backing, batting, and quilt top; baste.

2. Quilt as desired.

3. Attach a hanging sleeve, if desired.

4. Bind or finish as desired.

5. Attach a label.

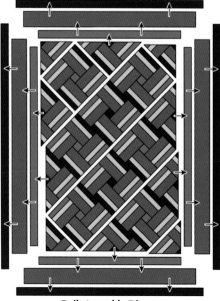
Quilt Assembly Diagram

October

PUMPKIN PATCH WALLHANGING

FINISHED PROJECT SIZE: 27^1/$_2$" x 46^1/$_2$"

FINISHED BLOCK SIZE: 8" x 8" and 7" x 7"

BLOCKS NEEDED: 4 Pumpkin blocks: 1 Block A, 1 Block B, 1 Block C , 1 Block D, and 4 Pumpkin Row blocks

One of our favorite fall activities is visiting a pumpkin patch and selecting just the right pumpkins for holiday decorating and cooking. Another favorite fall activity is to go to the local fabric shop and see all the new arrivals. We have selected 4 easy paper-pieced pumpkins for this project, and embellished them with 3-dimensional leaves and tendrils. Learn the basic steps for paper piecing any project, and some simple embellishment techniques that will add a new dimension to wall quilts.

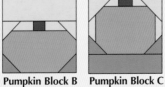

Pumpkin Block A   **Pumpkin Block B**   **Pumpkin Block C**   **Pumpkin Block D**   **Pumpkin Row Block**

MATERIALS

Sky blue: ^{1}/$_3$ yard for the Pumpkin blocks and background

Dark brown: Scrap or fat quarter for the Pumpkin blocks

Orange: ^{1}/$_3$ yard for the Pumpkin blocks

Dark green: 1 yard for the Pumpkin blocks, background, and leaves

Medium green: ^{5}/$_8$ yard for the leaves

Border print: 1 yard (add additional fabric for directional prints)

Backing: 1^1/$_2$ yards

Binding: ^{1}/$_2$ yard

Batting: 31" x 51"

Other materials: Green rayon thread, invisible nylon thread, lightweight paper for paper piecing, tear-away stabilizer, water-soluble stabilizer, plastic template material, fine-tip permanent marker, 1 package 32-gauge green cloth-wrapped wire (available at florist supply or craft stores), and spray starch

CUTTING

Prepare the fabric according to the instructions on page 11.

Light blue: Cut 2 rectangles 8^1/$_2$" x 5".

Dark green: Cut 2 rectangles 8^1/$_2$" x 5". Cut 4 squares 1^1/$_2$" x 1^1/$_2$" for the Pumpkin Row blocks.

Cut 2 rectangles 20" x 16" for the leaves.

Border print: Cut 3 strips 7¹/₂" wide, then cut into 2 strips 7¹/₂" x 32¹/₂" and 2 strips 7¹/₂" x 13".

Cut 4 strips 1¹/₂" wide, then cut into 8 squares 1¹/₂" x 1¹/₂", 8 rectangles 1¹/₂" x 3¹/₂", 8 rectangles 1¹/₂" x 5¹/₂", and 8 rectangles 1¹/₂" x 7¹/₂" for the Pumpkin Row blocks.

Medium green: Cut 2 rectangles 20" x 16" for the leaves.

Binding: Cut 5 strips 2¹/₂" wide.

BLOCK ASSEMBLY

Refer to page 14 for basic paper-piecing instructions.

1. Enlarge 200% and on pages 77–79 copy Pumpkin Blocks A, B, C, and D onto paper-piecing paper. Use a marker to write the color of each piece on the paper.

2. Follow the numerical order on the paper-piecing pattern to make Pumpkin Blocks A, B, and C. Paper piece each unit of Pumpkin Block D separately, then sew the units together as shown.

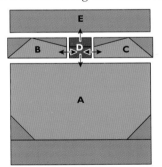

Pumpkin Block D Assembly Diagram

TIP *Press and spray starch the blocks before removing the paper.*

3. Remove the paper. Trim the blocks to 8¹/₂" x 8¹/₂".

WALLHANGING ASSEMBLY

1. Sew an 8¹/₂" x 5" blue strip to the top of Pumpkin Blocks A and D. Press.

2. Sew an 8¹/₂" x 5" dark green strip to the bottom of Blocks B and C. Press.

3. Sew the Pumpkin block units together as shown in the Wallhanging Assembly Diagram. Press.

BORDERS

Refer to the Essential Instructions on page 16.

1. Now is your chance to use up some extra scraps. Cut scraps into strips varying in width from 1" to 2", and at least 2" long. Piece the strips together alternating between green and brown or orange. You will need enough strip sets to total at least 12" long by at least 5¹/₂" wide. Trim to make the strip sets 5¹/₂" wide, and cut into 8 segments 1¹/₂" x 5¹/₂". Repeat to make strip sets 3¹/₂" wide, and cut 8 segments 1¹/₂" x 3¹/₂".

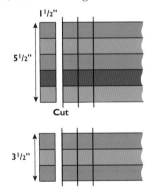

Sew leftover strips together and cut into segments.

2. Make 4 corner blocks, as shown in the Pumpkin Row Block Variation Assembly Diagram, using the strip set segments, the border print 1¹/₂" x 1¹/₂" squares, 1¹/₂" x 3¹/₂" rectangles, 1¹/₂" x 5 ¹/₂" rectangles, and 1¹/₂" x 7¹/₂" rectangles. Press.

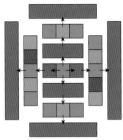

Pumpkin Row Block Assembly Diagram

3. Sew the top and bottom borders to the quilt top. Press.

4. Sew a Pumpkin Row block onto each end of the side border strips and press.

5. Add to the border/Pumpkin Row block units to the sides of the quilt top, matching seams and pinning. Press.

FINISHING

Refer to the Essential Instructions on page 17.

1. Layer the backing, batting, and quilt top; baste.

2. Quilt as desired.

3. Attach a hanging sleeve. Hand stitch after the embellishing is finished.

4. Bind or finish as desired.

5. Attach a label after the embellishing is complete.

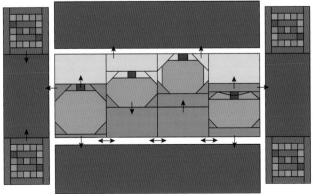

Wallhanging Assembly Diagram

EMBELLISHING

1. Enlarge 200% and trace the large and small leaf patterns onto the template material and cut out.

2. Pin the 2 dark green rectangles 20" x 16" right sides together. Use a marking pencil or pen to trace 4 small and 5 large leaves onto the fabric about ¹/₂" apart.

Trace the leaf.

3. Sew completely around the leaves on the marked line through both layers of fabric.

Sew on the line.

4. Cut out the leaves about ¹/₄" outside the stitching line. Trim all points to ¹/₈" from the stitching line, and clip seam allowances as necessary. Make a small slit in the back center of each leaf, and turn right side out. Press flat. Repeat this procedure for the medium green 20" x 16" rectangles to make 4 small and 7 large leaves.

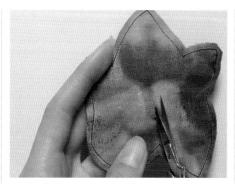

Slit the back to turn right side out.

5. Mark the stitching lines for the veins on the front of each leaf. Using stabilizer under the leaves, satin stitch the outer vein lines, then the center vein line. Remove stabilizer and press.

Satin stitch the veins.

6. Hand stitch to close the opening on the back of the leaves.

7. Using invisible nylon thread, attach the leaves to the quilt either by hand or by machine, stitching along the center vein, and one or two of the other veins.

8. Make the tendrils by placing a long (at least 5") piece of the wrapped floral wire on the water-soluble stabilizer. Use an open-toe presser foot and green rayon thread (on top and in the bobbin) to stitch over the top of the wire with a narrow satin stitch.

Satin stitch over the floral wire.

9. Gently pull the satin-stitched wire off of the stabilizer. Gently brush the wire with a damp cloth or cotton swab to remove any remaining stabilizer.

10. Wrap the wire around a pencil to create the curls. Make as many as desired. This project has 14 tendrils that vary in length from 5" to 9". Hand stitch these onto the quilt.

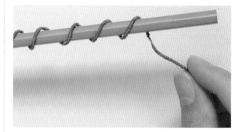

Wrap the wire around a pencil.

11. Hand stitch the hanging sleeve on the back of the quilt.

12. Attach a label.

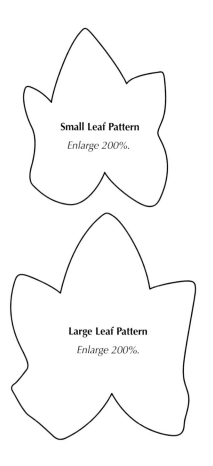

Small Leaf Pattern
Enlarge 200%.

Large Leaf Pattern
Enlarge 200%.

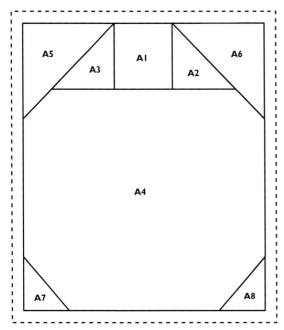

Pumpkin Block E Unit A
Enlarge 200%

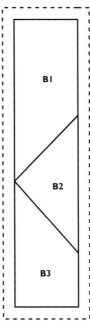

Pumpkin Block E Unit B
Enlarge 200%

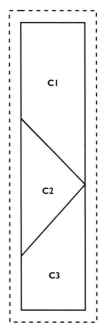

Pumpkin Block E Unit C
Enlarge 200%

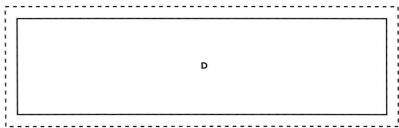

Pumpkin Block E Unit D
Enlarge 200%

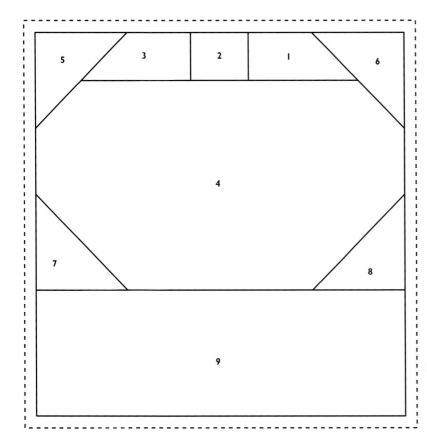

Pumpkin Block B
Version 2 for quilt
Enlarge 200%

November

Technique: Strip Piecing with Templates

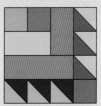

Vine Maple Leaf Block

FALLING LEAVES TABLE TOPPER

FINISHED PROJECT SIZE: 28" x 28"

FINISHED BLOCK SIZE: 6" x 6"

BLOCKS NEEDED: 4 Vine Maple Leaf blocks

F all is a season for crisp, clear mornings, bright blue skies, and the glorious colors of changing leaves. Nature provides the brilliance and variety of beautiful colors for quilters to interpret in their own way. Color selection and multiple half-square triangle piecing are the main focuses of this project. Pay particular attention to value, and how important dark, medium, and light fabrics are to this quilt. This project is beautiful for a table, and would also make a delightful small wallhanging.

MATERIALS

Pink: Scrap or fat quarter for the blocks

Rust: Scrap or fat quarter for the blocks

Yellow print: $3/8$ yard for the blocks and Border 2

Red: $3/8$ yard for the blocks and Border 3

Gold: Scrap or fat quarter for the triangles in the blocks

Dark brown: Scrap or fat quarter for the triangles in the blocks

Dark purple: Scrap or fat quarter for the triangles in the blocks

Light blue: $5/8$ yard for the blocks and Borders 1 and 4

Green: Scrap or fat quarter for the blocks

Binding: $3/8$ yard

Backing: 1 yard

Batting: 33" x 33"

CUTTING

Prepare the fabric according to the Essential Instructions on page 11.

Pink: Cut 4 squares 2" x 2" for the blocks.

Rust: Cut 4 squares 2" x 2" for the blocks.

Yellow print: Cut 4 rectangles 2" x 3½" for the blocks.

Border 2: Cut 2 strips 3½" wide, then cut into 2 strips 3½" x 15½" and 2 strips 3½" x 21½".

Red: Cut 4 strips 2" wide, then cut 1 strip into 4 rectangles 2" x 5" and 4 rectangles 2" x 3½" for the blocks.

Border 3: Cut the remaining strips into 2 strips 2" x 21½" and 2 strips 2" x 24½".

Gold: Cut 6 squares 2⅜" x 2⅜" for the half-square triangle units.

Dark brown: Cut 6 squares 2⅜" x 2⅜" for the half-square triangle units.

Dark purple: Cut 6 squares 2⅜" x 2⅜" for the half-square triangle units.

Light blue: Cut 6 squares 2⅜" x 2⅜" for the half-square triangle units.

Border 1: Cut 2 strips 2" wide, then cut into 2 strips 2" x 12½" and 2 strips 2" x 15½".

Border 4: Cut 4 strips 2½" wide, then cut into 2 strips 2½" x 24½", and 2 strips 2½" x 28½".

Green: Cut 4 squares 2" x 2" for the blocks.

Binding: Cut 4 strips 2½" wide.

BLOCK ASSEMBLY

Refer to the Essential Instructions on page 12.

1. Make the 4 Vine Maple Leaf block center units. Sew a pink square 2" x 2" to a rust square 2" x 2". Press. Sew a yellow strip 2" x 3½" onto the unit. Press. Sew a red strip 2" x 3½" onto the unit. Press. Add a red strip 2" x 5" and press.

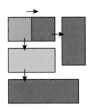

Vine Maple Leaf Block Center Assembly Diagram

2. Use the Quick Piecing Method (page 13) to make half-square triangle units. Using the 2⅜" squares, make 12 gold/dark brown and 12 dark purple/light blue 2" x 2" square unfinished units (1½" finished size). Press.

3. Sew 3 gold/brown half-square triangle units together as shown for each of the 4 blocks. Press. Sew 3 dark purple/light blue half-square triangle units together as shown for each of the 4 blocks. Press.

Note: The triangle units are assembled in a mirror image of each other.

Make 4 each.

4. Sew a gold/brown triangle unit onto one side of the center unit. Press. Sew a green 2" x 2" square onto the dark purple/light blue triangle unit. Press, then sew this strip onto the center unit. Press.

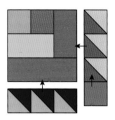

Vine Maple Leaf Block Assembly Diagram

TABLE TOPPER ASSEMBLY

1. Sew the 4 blocks together as shown in the Table Topper Assembly Diagram. Press.

2. Sew the Border 1 side strips, then the top and bottom strips, to the center block unit. Press.

3. Add Borders 2, 3, and 4 in the same manner.

FINISHING

Refer to the Essential Instructions on page 17.

1. Layer the backing, batting, and quilt top; baste.

2. Quilt as desired.

3. Attach a hanging sleeve if desired.

4. Bind or finish as desired.

5. Attach a label.

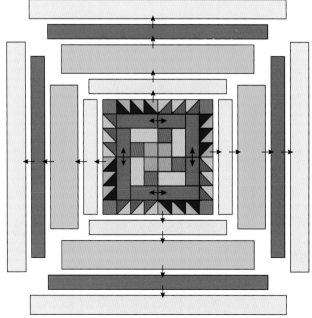

Table Topper Assembly Diagram

Falling Leaves Quilt

FINISHED QUILT SIZE: 60" x 60"

FINISHED BLOCK SIZE: 6" x 6" and 12" x 12"

BLOCKS NEEDED: 30 Vine Maple Leaf blocks, 6 Large Maple Leaf blocks, and 2 Half Large Maple Leaf blocks (12" x 6")

Floating leaves in a gentle breeze on a clear autumn day inspired this quilt. Learn how quickly multiple half-square triangle units can be made. This quilt integrates different sizes of blocks to easily create a complex look.

Vine Maple Leaf Block

Large Maple Leaf Block

FABRIC SELECTION TIPS

Select a light blue background fabric that suggests the appearance of floating clouds. Look for a yellow with a large-scale print for the squares. All other fabrics should be medium to dark value. Select the medium to dark blue and purple triangle fabrics next, then the bright red, oranges, and browns. Finally, select the green for the squares. A dark blue binding finishes the quilt.

MATERIALS

Pink: Large scrap or fat quarter for the Vine Maple Leaf blocks

Rust: $1/2$ yard for the Vine Maple Leaf and Large Maple Leaf blocks

Yellow Print: $1^1/4$ yards for the Vine Maple Leaf, Large Maple Leaf, plain blocks, and strips

Red: $1/2$ yard for the Vine Maple Leaf blocks

Gold: $2/3$ yard for the Vine Maple Leaf and Large Maple Leaf blocks

Dark brown: $1/3$ yard for the Vine Maple Leaf and Large Maple Leaf blocks

Dark purple: $3/4$ yard for the Vine Maple Leaf and Large Maple Leaf blocks

Dark green: Large scrap or fat quarter for the Large Maple Leaf blocks

Medium green: Large scrap or fat quarter for the Vine Maple Leaf blocks

Dark blue: $1/3$ yard for the Large Maple Leaf blocks

Medium blue: $1/3$ yard for the Large Maple Leaf blocks

Light blue: $1^1/2$ yards for the Vine Maple Leaf blocks and setting strips

Binding: $5/8$ yard

Backing: $3^1/2$ yards

Batting: 65" x 65"

Spray starch

CUTTING

Prepare the fabric according to the Essential Instructions on page 11.

Pink: Cut 2 strips 2" wide, then cut into 30 squares 2" x 2" for the Vine Maple Leaf blocks.

Rust: Cut 3 strips $2^3/8$" wide for the half-square triangle units.

Cut 2 strips 2" wide, then cut into 30 squares 2" x 2" for the Vine Maple Leaf blocks.

Yellow print: Cut 1 square $10^1/4$", then cut diagonally twice for the Half Large Maple Leaf blocks.

Cut 2 strips $6^7/8$" wide, then cut into 6 squares $6^7/8$" x $6^7/8$" for the Large Maple Leaf blocks.

Cut 1 strip $6^1/2$" wide, then cut into 2 strips $6^1/2$" x $12^1/2$" (A15, B23) and 1 square $6^1/2$" x $6^1/2$" (B17).

Cut 3 strips 2" wide, then cut into 30 rectangles 2" x $3^1/2$" for the Vine Maple Leaf blocks.

Red: Cut 7 strips 2" wide, then cut into 30 rectangles 2" x $3^1/2$" and 30 rectangles 2" x 5" for the Vine Maple Leaf blocks.

Gold: Cut 6 strips $2^3/8$" wide for the half-square triangle units.

Dark brown: Cut 3 strips $2^3/8$" wide for the half-square triangle units.

Dark purple: Cut 1 strip $5^3/8$" long, then cut into 7 squares $5^3/8$" x $5^3/8$". Cut the squares diagonally to make 14 triangles for the Large Maple Leaf blocks.

Cut 6 strips $2^3/8$" wide for the half-square triangle units.

Dark green: Cut 2 strips 2" wide, then cut into 28 squares 2" x 2" for the Large Maple Leaf blocks.

Medium green: Cut 2 strips 2" wide, then cut into 30 squares 2" x 2" for the Vine Maple Leaf blocks.

Dark blue: Cut 1 strip $5^3/8$" wide, then cut into 7 squares $5^3/8$" x $5^3/8$". Cut the squares diagonally to make 14 triangles for the Large Maple Leaf blocks.

Medium blue: Cut 3 strips $2^3/8$" wide for the half-square triangle units.

Light blue: Cut 6 strips $6^1/2$" wide, sew into one long strip and cut the following: 1 strip $6^1/2$" x $48^1/2$" (D7); 1 strip $6^1/2$" x $42^1/2$" (C1); 3 strips $6^1/2$" x $24^1/2$" (C3, D1, D4); 1 strip $6^1/2$" x $18^1/2$" (B18); 2 strips $6^1/2$" x $12^1/2$" (A5, C5); and 3 squares $6^1/2$" x $6^1/2$" (A3, A6, A16).

Cut 3 strips $2^3/8$" wide for the half-square triangle units.

Binding: Cut 7 strips $2^1/2$" wide for binding.

BLOCK ASSEMBLY

1. Use the Quick Piecing Method on page 13 to make half-square triangle units. Use the gold $2^3/8$" strips and the brown $2^3/8$" strips to make 90 gold/brown half-square triangle units.

Make 90 light blue/dark purple half-square triangle units in the same manner. Use these for the Vine Maple Leaf blocks.

Make 84 gold/rust and 84 medium blue/dark purple half-square triangle units for the Large Maple Leaf blocks in the same manner. Press towards the dark fabric.

2. Use the gold/brown and the light blue/dark purple half-square triangle units to make 30 Vine Maple Leaf blocks. Refer to page 81 for the block assembly.

3. To make the Large Maple Leaf block center, sew 4 purple $5^3/8"$ triangles onto a yellow square $6^7/8"$ x $6^7/8"$. Press. Make 3 blocks. Repeat using the blue $5^3/8"$ triangles. Make 3 blocks.

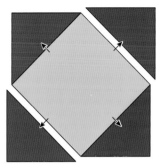

Large Maple Leaf Block Center Assembly Diagram

4. Make the Half Large Maple Leaf block center by sewing 2 of the purple $5^3/8"$ triangles onto a yellow $10^1/4"$ triangle. Press. Repeat using 2 blue $5^3/8"$ triangles.

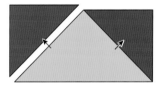

Half Large Maple Leaf Block Center Assembly Diagram

5. Sew 3 gold/rust half-square triangle units and 3 medium blue/purple half-square triangle units together. Press. Make 26 strips. Note: The triangle units are assembled in a mirror image of each other.

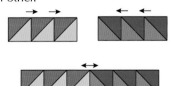

6. Sew a half-square triangle unit strip to each side of the Large Maple Leaf block center unit. Press.

7. Sew a 2" dark green square onto each side of 14 half-square triangle unit strips. Press. Sew 12 of these strips onto the bottom and top of the Large Maple Leaf block center unit. Press.

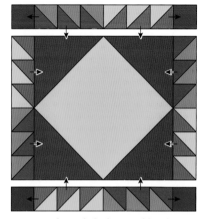

Large Maple Leaf Block Assembly Diagram

8. Make 2 Half Large Maple Leaf blocks using 2 gold/rust and 2 blue/purple triangle units, and 2 square/triangle strip units. Press.

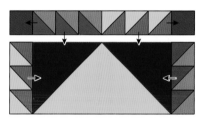

Half Large Maple Leaf Block Assembly Diagram

QUILT ASSEMBLY

1. This quilt is not sewn in rows, but is very easy to put together. Lay out all of the blocks and light blue pieces in units as shown in the Quilt Assembly Diagram. Press all seams open.

2. Sew the units together.

Sew A1, A2, and A3 together.

Sew A4 to A5. Sew A6 to A7, and sew this unit to A8.

Sew the A4–5 unit to the A6–8 unit.

Sew the A1–3 unit to the A4–8 unit.

Sew A10, A11, A12, and A13 together; and sew this unit to A9.

Sew A14, A15, and A16 together; sew this unit onto the A9–13 unit. Sew the two A units together.

3. Sew B2, B3, B4, and B5 together; sew this unit to B1 and B6.

Sew B7, B8, B9, and B10 together; sew this unit to B11.

Sew B12, B13, B14, and B15 together; then sew this unit to the B7–11 unit.

Sew B16, B17, and B18 together; then sew units B1–6, B7–15, and B16–18 together.

Sew B19, B20, B21, and B22 together, then sew this unit to B23. Add B24.

Sew the 2 B units together.

4. Sew C1 to C2, then sew onto the left side.

Sew C3, C4 and C5 together, then sew onto the right side.

5. Sew D1, D2, D3, and D4 together, then sew this onto the top.

Sew D5, D6, and D7 together, then sew this unit onto the bottom.

FINISHING

Refer to the Essential Instructions on page 17.

1. Layer the backing, batting, and quilt top; baste.

2. Quilt as desired.

3. Attach a hanging sleeve if desired.

4. Bind or finish as desired.

5. Attach a label.

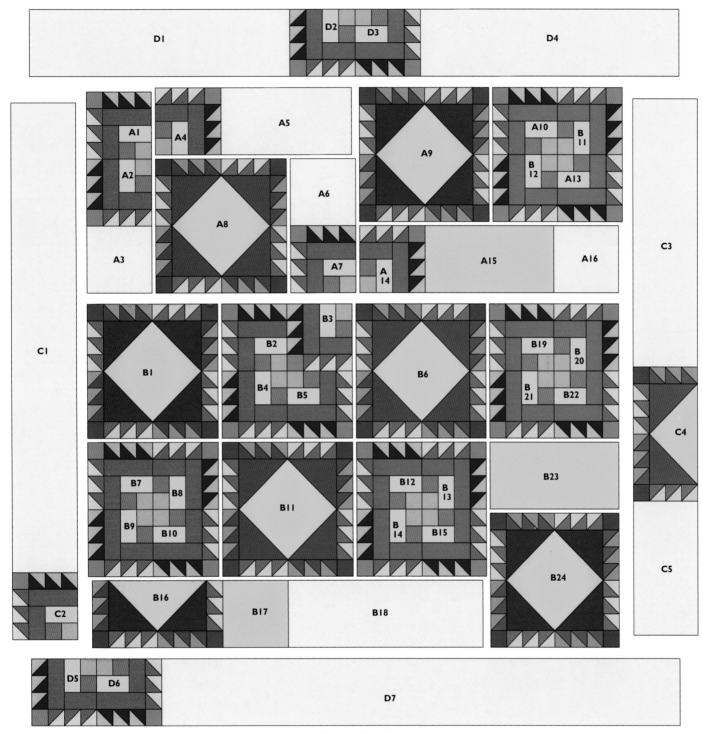

Quilt Assembly Diagram

December

Technique: Strip Piecing, Paper Piecing, and Machine Appliqué

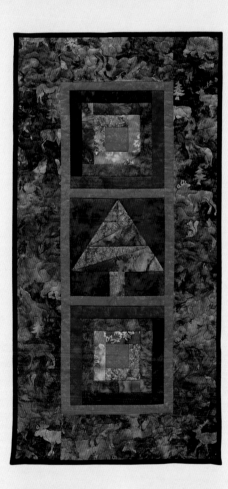

Northwoods Door Hanger

FINISHED PROJECT SIZE: $18^1/2$" x $36^1/2$"

FINISHED BLOCK SIZE: 8" x 8"

BLOCKS NEEDED: 2 Log Cabin blocks and 1 Evergreen block

Christmas trees and Log Cabins remind us of the comfort of home and family. This seasonal door hanger is perfect for a one-day beginner class. Log Cabin blocks and a paper-pieced Evergreen block complete this hanger. Learn easy strip piecing and paper piecing to complete this project.

MATERIALS

Red: $1/4$ yard for log center and the inner border

Light green: Large scrap or fat quarter for the Evergreen block and Log Cabin blocks

Medium green: Large scrap or fat quarter for the Evergreen block and Log Cabin blocks

Dark green: Large scrap or fat quarter for the Log Cabin blocks

Light maroon: Large scrap or fat quarter for the Log Cabin blocks

Medium maroon: Large scrap or fat quarter for the Log Cabin blocks

Dark maroon: Large scrap or fat quarter for the Log Cabin blocks

Blue: Large scrap or fat quarter for the Evergreen block background

Brown: Scrap or fat quarter for the Evergreen block trunk

Border print: $1/2$ yard for the outer border

Binding: $3/8$ yard

Backing: $7/8$ yard

Batting: 22" x 40"

Other materials: Lightweight paper for paper piecing, fine-tip permanent marker, and spray starch

CUTTING

Prepare the fabric according to the Essential Instructions on page 11.

Red: Cut 1 strip $2^1/2$" wide, then cut into 2 squares $2^1/2$" x $2^1/2$" for the Log Cabin center.

Inner border: Cut 3 strips $1^1/2$" wide, then cut into 2 strips $1^1/2$" x $28^1/2$" and 4 strips $1^1/2$" x $8^1/2$".

Light green: Cut 1 strip $1^1/2$" wide for the Log Cabin blocks.

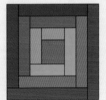

Log Cabin Block

Evergreen Block

Medium green: Cut 1 strip 1¹/₂" wide for the Log Cabin blocks.

Dark green: Cut 1 strip 1¹/₂" wide for the Log Cabin blocks.

Light maroon: Cut 1 strip 1¹/₂" wide for the Log Cabin blocks.

Medium maroon: Cut 1 strip 1¹/₂" wide for the Log Cabin blocks.

Dark maroon: Cut 1 strip 1¹/₂" wide for the Log Cabin blocks.

Outer border print: Cut 3 strips 4¹/₂" wide, then cut into 2 strips 4¹/₂" x 10¹/₂" and 2 strips 4¹/₂" x 36¹/₂".

Binding: Cut 4 strips 2¹/₂" wide.

BLOCK ASSEMBLY

Refer to the Essential Instructions on page 12.

Log Cabin Block

1. Make the 2 Log Cabin blocks. Place a light green 1¹/₂" wide strip on top of a red 2¹/₂" x 2¹/₂" square with right sides together. Stitch, then trim the strip even with the square. Press.

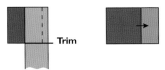

Piece the center.

2. Turn the center square ¹/₄ turn to the left. Place a strip of light green on the piece, stitch, and trim. Press.

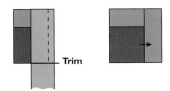

Turn the center square and add the next log.

⊞ **TIP** *Rotate the block so the previously sewn log is on top. After the first three colors are sewn on, you will always be sewing over 2 seams.*

3. Repeat Step 2, adding the light maroon print to the next 2 sides of the center square. Press.

Add light maroon.

4. Continue alternating green and maroon strips until there are 3 strips on each side of the red center. Make 2 Log Cabin blocks.

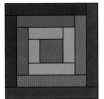

Finished block, make 2.

Evergreen Block

Refer to the Essential Instructions on page 14.

1. Enlarge 200% the Evergreen block pattern on page 92, and make 1 copy on paper-piecing paper. Use the marker to write the color of each piece on the paper to make the piecing easier. Remember, the paper piecing patterns are mirror-imaged, so mark the paper-piecing patterns accordingly.

2. Following the numerical order on the pattern and the coloration shown in the assembly diagram, paper piece the Evergreen block tree and trunk units separately. Sew the units together. Press.

DOOR HANGER ASSEMBLY

1. Lay out the door hanger as shown in the Assembly Diagram.

2. Sew the 1¹/₂" x 8¹/₂" inner border sashing strips to the tops of all the blocks and to the bottom of one Log Cabin block. Press.

3. Sew the blocks together. Press.

4. Sew the inner border side sashing to each side of the door hanger. Press.

5. Add the outer border strips to the top and bottom, then to each side. Press.

FINISHING

Refer to the Essential Instructions on page 17.

1. Layer the backing, batting, and quilt top; baste.

2. Quilt as desired.

3. Attach a hanging sleeve.

4. Bind or finish as desired.

5. Attach a label.

⊞ **TIP** *For a decorative finish, place a small rod in the sleeve pocket; make it long enough to extend beyond the door hanger edges. Tie a 1" wide or wider ribbon to each end of the rod, then tie together with a bow. Use a Christmas wreath holder to hang the door hanger.*

Door Hanger Assembly Diagram

Northwood's Quilt

FINISHED QUILT SIZE: $62\frac{1}{2}"$ x $62\frac{1}{2}"$

FINISHED BLOCK SIZE: 8" x 8" Log Cabin and Evergreen blocks, and 14" x 14" Square-in-a-Square block

BLOCKS NEEDED: 8 Log Cabin, 4 Evergreen, and 1 Square-in-a-Square

This quilt is reminiscent of a cozy winter evening spent snuggled up by the fireplace with a mug of hot chocolate. What better way to complement evergreen trees and Log Cabins than to add a moose, bear, and fish to this quilt? The project is pieced using easy strip piecing, paper piecing, and machine appliqué.

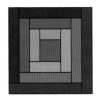
Log Cabin block

Evergreen block

Square-in-a-Square block

FABRIC SELECTION TIPS

The border print was the inspiration for this quilt. The rich browns, maroons, and greens were suggested by the warm earthy tones of the Bali print. The light fabric is a multi-toned Bali with all the quilt colors in it. The blue is a great background to the tree block, and lends a soothing element to the quilt. A red was chosen for the traditional center of the Log Cabin. The blue and red of the borders add balance to the quilt.

MATERIALS

Red: $^1/_2$ yard for the Log Cabin blocks and Outer Border 2

Light green: $^1/_2$ yard for the Evergreen and Log Cabin blocks

Medium green: $^1/_2$ yard for the Evergreen and Log Cabin blocks

Dark green: $^1/_4$ yard for the Log Cabin blocks

Light maroon: $^1/_4$ yard for the Log Cabin blocks

Medium maroon: $^1/_2$ yard for the Log Cabin and center Square-in-a-Square blocks

Dark maroon: $^1/_4$ yard for the Log Cabin blocks

Blue: $^7/_8$ yard for the Evergreen block background and Outer Border 1

Brown: Large scrap or fat quarter for the Evergreen block

Assorted light greens: $^1/_2$ yard total for the Diamond Border

Assorted dark greens: $^3/_4$ yard total for the Diamond Border

Beige: 1 yard for the center Square-in-a-Square block, Diamond Border, and corners

Border print: $1^5/_8$ yards for Inner Border 1, Inner Border 2, and Outer Border 3

Black: $^1/_4$ yard for the appliqué

Binding: $^5/_8$ yard

Backing: $3^3/_4$ yards

Batting: 67" x 67"

Other materials: Lightweight paper for paper piecing, tear-away stabilizer, and fine-tip permanent marker

CUTTING

Prepare the fabric according to the Essential Instructions on page 11.

Red: Cut 1 strip $2^1/_2$" wide, then cut into 8 squares $2^1/_2$" x $2^1/_2$" wide for the Log Cabin center.

Outer Border 2: Cut 5 strips $1^1/_2$" wide. Sew into one long strip, then cut into 2 strips $1^1/_2$" x $48^1/_2$" and 2 strips $1^1/_2$" x $50^1/_2$".

Light green: Cut 2 strips $1^1/_2$" wide for the Log Cabin blocks.

Medium green: Cut 3 strips $1^1/_2$" wide for the Log Cabin blocks.

Dark green: Cut 3 strips $1^1/_2$" wide for the Log Cabin blocks.

Light maroon: Cut 2 strips $1^1/_2$" wide for the Log Cabin blocks.

Medium maroon: Cut 3 strips $1^1/_2$" wide for the Log Cabin blocks.

Cut 2 square $8^3/_8$" x $8^3/_8$", then cut in half diagonally to make 4 triangles for the center Square-in-a-Square.

Dark maroon: Cut 4 strips $1^1/_2$" wide for the Log Cabin blocks.

Blue: Outer Border 1: Cut 5 strips $2^1/_2$" wide. Sew into one long strip, then cut into 2 strips $2^1/_2$" x $44^1/_2$" and 2 strips $2^1/_2$" x $48^1/_2$".

Assorted light greens: Cut 2 strips $5^1/_2$" wide, then cut into 8 A diamond pieces using the enlarged pattern on page 93 for the Diamond Border.

Assorted dark greens: Cut 4 strips $3^1/_2$" wide, then cut into 16 B triangle pieces using the enlarged pattern on page 93 for the Diamond Border.

Cut 2 strips $3^1/_4$" wide. Cut into 8 rectangles $3^1/_4$" x $6^7/_8$", then cut diagonally as shown to make 16 end triangles for the Diamond Border.

Cutting left bottom and right top corner triangle, cut 4 each.

Cutting left top and right bottom corner triangles, cut 4 each.

> **⊞ TIP** *Enlarge and trace the diamond pattern on page 93 on paper; cut out the diamond shape from the center of the paper. Use the resulting paper window to view the fabric pieces as they will appear in the quilt.*

Beige: Cut 1 square $10^3/_8$ x $10^3/_8$" for the center Square-in-a-Square.

Cut 1 strip $5^1/_2$" wide, then cut into 4 squares $5^1/_2$" x $5^1/_2$" for the Diamond Border corners.

Cut 2 strips $5^1/_2$" wide. Use the strips and cut 4 A diamond pieces using the enlarged pattern on page 93 for the Diamond Border.

Border print: Inner Border 1: Cut 2 strips $1^1/2$" wide, then cut into 2 strips $1^1/2$" x $14^1/2$" and 2 strips $1^1/2$" x $16^1/2$".

Inner Border 2: Cut 4 strips $1^1/2$" wide, then cut into 2 strips $1^1/2$" x $32^1/2$" and 2 strips $1^1/2$" x $34^1/2$".

Outer Border 3: Cut 6 strips $6^1/2$" wide. Sew into one long strip, then cut into 2 strips $6^1/2$" x $50^1/2$" and 2 strips $6^1/2$" x $62^1/2$".

Black: Enlarge 200% and trace appliqué patterns on page 92 to the paper side of the paper-backed adhesive. Cut 1 moose, 4 fish, 2 bears and 2 bears reversed.

Binding: Cut 7 strips $2^1/2$" wide.

BLOCK ASSEMBLY

1. Refer to page 87 to make 8 Log Cabin blocks and 4 Evergreen blocks. Set aside.

2. Make the center Square-in-a-Square block. Sew 4 medium maroon triangles to the beige center square $10^3/8$" x $10^3/8$". Press. Trim the block to $14^1/2$" x $14^1/2$".

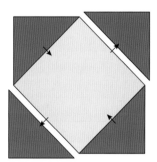

Making the Square-in-a-Square block

3. Add Inner Border 1 strips to each side of the center block, then to the top and bottom. Press. Set aside.

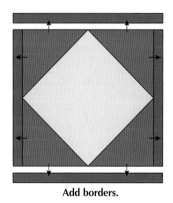

Add borders.

DIAMOND BORDER

1. Sew a dark green left top triangle to a light green A diamond, then sew to a dark green B triangle. Make 4 Left Units. Spray starch and press.

2. Sew 2 dark green B triangles to a beige A diamond. Make 4 Middle Units. Spray starch and press.

3. Sew a dark green B triangle to a light green A diamond, then sew to a dark green right bottom triangle. Make 4 Right Units. Spray starch and press.

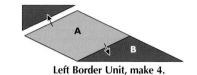

Left Border Unit, make 4.

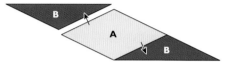

Middle Border Unit, make 4.

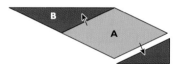

Right Border Unit, make 4.

4. Assemble the Diamond border. Match seams and sew together. Spray starch and press. Make 4 units.

Border Assembly

QUILT ASSEMBLY

1. Lay out all the blocks as shown in the Quilt Assembly Diagram, noting the orientation of the blocks.

2. Sew 2 Log Cabin blocks together to make a left side unit. Press. Repeat for the right side. Sew to the Center Moose unit. Press.

3. Sew 2 Log Cabin blocks and 2 Evergreen blocks together to make a top unit. Press. Repeat for the bottom. Sew to the Center Moose unit. Press.

4. Add Inner Border 2 strips to each side of the Center Moose unit, then the top and bottom borders. Press.

5. Sew a side Diamond Border to each side of the center unit. Press.

6. Sew 2 beige 5½" x 5½" squares to each end of the top and bottom Diamond Border. Sew to the center unit. Press.

7. Add Outer Borders 1, 2 and 3, in the same manner as Inner Border 2.

APPLIQUÉ

Refer to the Essential Instructions on page 15.

1. Refer to the quilt photo for placement of the moose, bears and fish. Fuse to the appropriate squares and diamonds.

2. Place tear-away stabilizer under each shape. Machine-stitch around the edges of all the pieces using a straight stitch.

FINISHING

Refer to the Essential Instructions on pages 17.

1. Layer the backing, batting, and quilt top; baste.

2. Quilt as desired.

3. Attach a hanging sleeve, if desired.

4. Bind or finish as desired.

5. Attach a label.

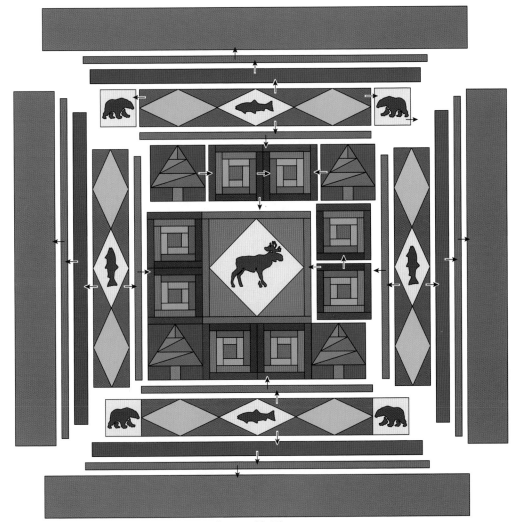

Quilt Assembly Diagram

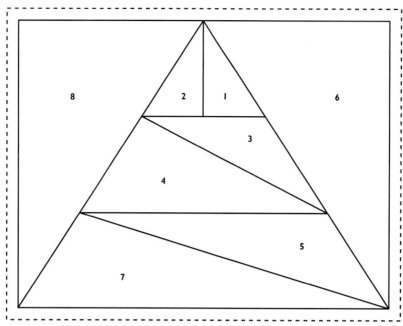

Evergreen Block Tree Unit
Enlarge 200%

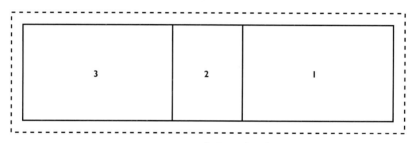

Evergreen Block Trunk Unit
Enlarge 200%

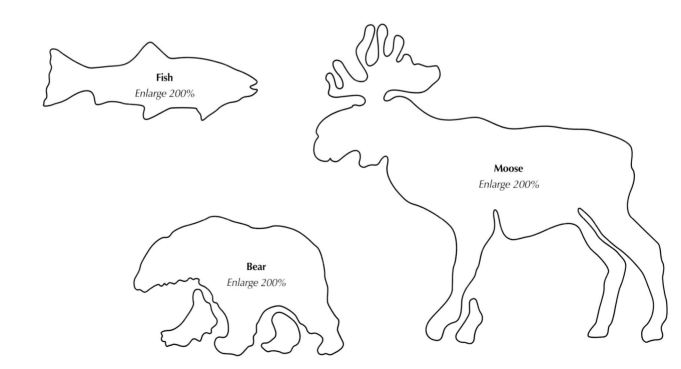

Fish
Enlarge 200%

Moose
Enlarge 200%

Bear
Enlarge 200%

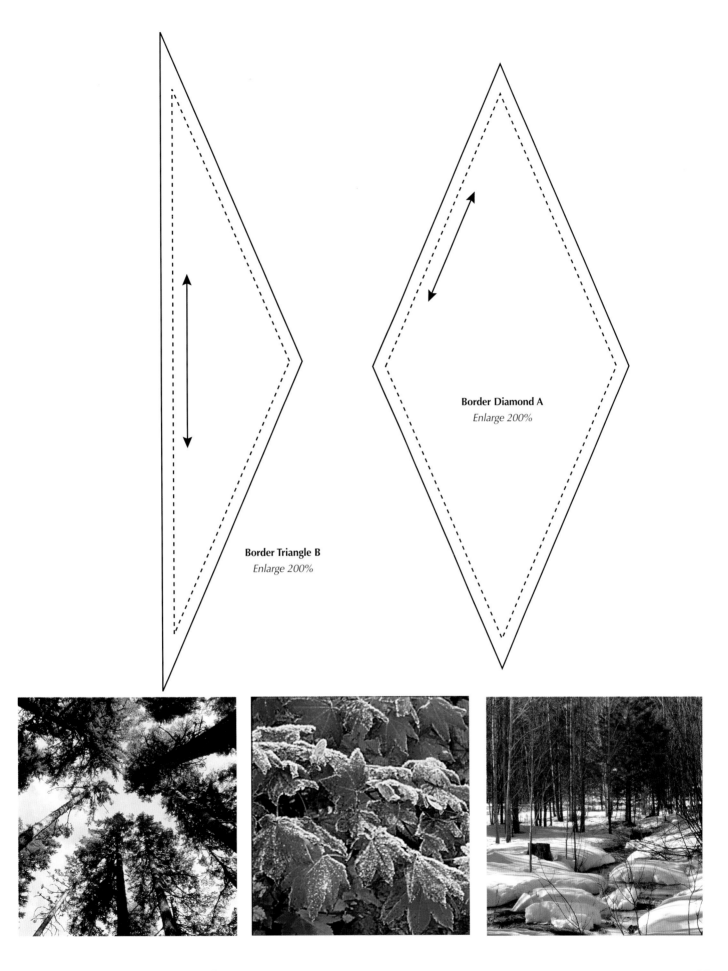

Border Triangle B
Enlarge 200%

Border Diamond A
Enlarge 200%

About the Authors

The high-desert town of Bend, Oregon, is the home of Barbara Baker, who is always in the midst of a creative whirlwind. She sews, quilts, paints, buys fabric, gardens, and attends many hockey tournaments. An active member of the Mount Bachelor Quilting Guild, Barbara designed the guild's logo.

Barbara creates quilts for Robert Kaufmann Fabrics, and her quilts have been published in *McCall's Quilting* magazine. Her quilts have also appeared in several C&T titles, including *Diane Phalen Quilts, Laurel Burch Quilts, and Wine Country Quilts.*

Designing and teaching at local quilt shops and guilds, and at the Quilter's Affair in Sisters, Oregon, help to enrich Barbara's quiltmaking skills. She loves to experiment and try new techniques, colors, and designs. Barbara is also a professional longarm machine quilter, and incorporates that expertise in her work.

Jeri creates beautiful quilts and other artwork in the high-desert town of Bend, Oregon. She started quilting over 20 years ago. Jeri has taken tailoring and numerous art courses at the college level, and uses her artistic skills when designing and making quilts and clothing.

Jeri is a CPA and has a degree in Computer Information Systems. She creates hand-dyed and painted fabrics and threads and enjoys creating her own quilt designs and patterns. Jeri uses a variety of computer programs to assist in generating designs. She is a passionate photographer, and often uses her photographs as inspirations for her work.

Jeri's photographs and/or quilts have been published in several C&T titles, including *Laurel Burch Quilts* and *Wine Country Quilts.* She has taught at quilt shops and guilds, and at the Quilter's Affair in Sisters, Oregon. When Jeri is not creating quilts, she enjoys spending time with her husband and family and going on outdoor adventures. She may be found hiking, biking, snowshoeing, or rafting, often with her camera in tow just looking for the next inspiration.

OTHER FINE BOOKS FROM C&T PUBLISHING

Index